A **NON**–FREAKED OUT GUIDE TO TEACHING THE **COMMON CORE**

USING THE 32 LITERACY ANCHOR STANDARDS TO DEVELOP COLLEGE- AND CAREER-READY STUDENTS

Dave Stuart Jr.

JB JOSSEY-BASS™
A Wiley Brand

Cover Illustration: © davorr/istockphoto
Cover Concept: Heather Hazard

Published by Jossey-Bass
A Wiley Brand
One Montgomery Street, Suite 1200, San Francisco, CA 94104-4594—www.josseybass.com

Jossey-Bass books and products are available through most bookstores. To contact Jossey-Bass directly call our Customer Care Department within the U.S. at 800-956-7739, outside the U.S. at 317-572-3986, or fax 317-572-4002.

Wiley publishes in a variety of print and electronic formats and by print-on-demand. Some material included with standard print versions of this book may not be included in ebooks or in print-on-demand. If this book refers to media such as a CD or DVD that is not included in the version you purchased, you may download this material at http://booksupport.wiley.com. For more information about Wiley products, visit www.wiley.com.

Library of Congress Cataloging-in-Publication Data is on file.

ISBN 978-1-118-95226-9 (paperback)
ISBN 978-1-118-95227-6 (ebk.)
ISBN 978-1-118-95228-3 (ebk.)

Printed in the United States of America
FIRST EDITION
PB Printing   10 9 8 7 6 5 4 3 2 1

CONTENTS

PART II: THE ANCHOR STANDARDS IN READING

PART III: THE ANCHOR STANDARDS IN WRITING

PART IV: THE ANCHOR STANDARDS IN SPEAKING AND LISTENING

PART V: THE ANCHOR STANDARDS IN LANGUAGE

For Jesus and Crystal

PREFACE

The first time I thought about creating a blog around the Common Core, it was for two reasons: First, even back in spring 2012 I, as a full-time English and social studies high school teacher, was sensing the freaking out that, like some kind of psychotic midwife, attended the Common Core's entry into the world. Second, I was curious to see what all the freaking out was about. This curiosity was quickly frustrated, however, by a dearth of down-to-earth, straightforward treatments of the standards. I simply could not find any solid, helpful, approachable information. And so I, a guy who had no idea what the Common Core State Standards actually said, started a blog called *Teaching the Core* with the intent of simply reading through the document and writing about what I read.

Yet something funny happened as I read and wrote and interacted with a growing number of teachers online around the topic of these learning goals: I started becoming passionate about the wasteful cost that the Common Core

freak out was inflicting on the U.S. education reform discussion. I saw a lot of energy getting spent on negative tweets and articles and blogs and conversations and rants, and, to make matters worse, very little of this negativity actually lined up with what the standards contained! It was becoming apparent that many folks hadn't even *read* the standards (or, if they had, they hadn't understood much). It reminded me of religious adherents who, rather than reading or reflecting on their religious texts, believe fervently in their preconceptions and then use either real or imagined parts of the texts to support what they already believed to start with.

And so I came to advocate for and write about a "non–freaked out approach" to the Common Core. This grew out of a desire to serve those educators and parents and policymakers who refuse to freak out while pursuing the greatest aim of education: the long-term flourishing of human beings. If you are committed to remaining focused on that central aim, casting away anything that gets in the way of long-term student flourishing, even if that is your educational philosophy or bias or comfort zone or pet lesson, then this book, my friend, has been a labor of love for you.

I do hope it helps. If I can be of any additional service to you, please be in touch through www.teachingthecore .com/contact-dave.

DAVE STUART JR.

ACKNOWLEDGMENTS

What you hold in your hand is a book (crazy, right?), and books are generally these audacious collaborations of people who all chip in to communicate a thing. And although you can decide, based on the pages that follow, how well I've done at communicating the thing, I want to take a couple of pages now to make one thing very clear: anything helpful or encouraging you read here is entirely due to the people I'm about to thank. This book, my first, wouldn't exist at all if it weren't for some of them, and it wouldn't be *worth* existing if it weren't for all of them.

First, as a kid, I started dreaming of writing books, and because of people like my grandparents—Dean and Carol Stuart, Bud and Murt LaJoye, Donna and Norval Sinclair, Jack and Gloria Burg—and my parents—Dave and Kathy Stuart, Brian and Lisa Sinclair—my dreams, little sparks at the time, were allowed to catch fire. Thank you all for showing me what it means to work humble and work hard; if you hadn't taught me these things, I wouldn't be

much of a teacher, writer, husband, or friend.

I have more close family members who give me much cause for joy and gratitude, without which my writing would be flat: my parents-in-law, Bill and Sylvia Edwards; my siblings, by blood and by marriage (I forget the difference most times), Mel-Dawg and Brandon Krieg, Nicko and Amber Edwards, Adam and Benjibu-san Sinclair, and Brooke Edwards; and the three most inside-and-out gorgeous little girls ever: Hadassah Ellen, Laura Lindsay, and Marlena Grace. You've all taught me better how to laugh with and relate to and love on people, and I hope that comes through in how I write.

Then there are the people who, despite no blood or legal connection, have irrevocably made their mark on my life as mentors; without these people, you wouldn't hold a book in your hand, because I wouldn't be driven by such a desire to imitate them, their excellence, and their service to others: Laura VanRyn and Lindsay Veitch taught me to be a joyful servant; Brian Scriven taught me to be bold and visionary; Trent Gladstone taught me the holiness of striving for excellence in the workplace; and Tim Knapp pushed me to find ways to use my gifts outside of the classroom.

A few key people at the University of Michigan helped shaped me into an eager, semi-able first-year teacher: Joyce Sutton, you made my transition from pre-med to pre-ed as painless as possible (you were also so kind to me about my admissions essay); Christian Dallavis, Vicki Haviland, and Anne Ruggles Gere, you are the best ed profs ever; Deborah Ball, you received an impassioned email from me and, despite being a busy dean, took the time to sit with me and chat about it. Thank you all for your investments in me.

You don't write well about teaching unless you've spent years doing it, and my years in teaching would have been pointless apart from the influence of educators. At Woodlawn Middle School of Baltimore, Maryland, where I began my career, I am indebted to so many of you: Wilson, Frazier, Salipata, Skinner, King, Benedetto, Jones, Maul, Ingram, Oliver, Zamarron, Strother, Newman, Prioleau, Dixon, Longstreet, and Clarkie-Clark. I don't understand why you treated me as kindly as you did,

but I am a better teacher and a better man because of your influence. Again, thank you to my first head principal, Brian Scriven: you took me under your wing like a son—you, sir, taught me to pick up garbage in the hallways; you brought me suit shopping after church one Sunday; you showed me what it can look like to give sacrificially and fully in a public school; and you spoke to me about the book I might someday write. I didn't know it would be about this, but I haven't given up on it, thanks to you. Thank you for your mentorship in a critical stage of my professional life.

Before moving to Michigan, I lived in New York City for a year, and I owe much to the people of the 42nd Street Capital Grille, the 168th Street Starbucks, Ross Global Academy, Atrium Staffing, and *Youthworker Journal*, all of whom employed me at the same time and were therefore patient as I learned to juggle multiple jobs at once. If it weren't for your kindness toward me, I would never be able to teach and write and business and dad and husband with a modicum of competence.

When I did move to Michigan, I arrogantly thought that my three years of teaching experience would guarantee me a job anywhere I wanted, and I wanted to be in an urban school in Grand Rapids. Confoundingly to me at the time but thankfully to me now, I was humbled during that season of job searching and ended up a long-term substitute in Cedar Springs (thanks, in huge part, to the Tackmann family, who believed in me before ever meeting me). This district is home to another group of educators who have shaped me significantly. I am indebted to many people in the Cedar Springs Public Schools, most especially those whom I work with frequently. To Ron, who hired me; to Doug, who taught me to value instructional time; to Painter, who forces me to think and graciously gives me rides to school in the winter; to Steve Seward, who nudged me to offer teacher workshops; to the English professional learning community (PLC), who intimidated me with their excellence; to Amy, who recommended that I join the Lake Michigan Writing Project; to Scott Hazel, who invited me to Spring Hill; to Anne, who dealt with my book-writing crazy; to Ken and April, who dealt with my inexperience when I was a total newb in Cedar Springs; to the social studies PLC, who put up with me during my first year in the group, and who still do; to Sairah, who deals with my crankiness—thank you all. I've saved one group of Cedar Springs High School people for last because of how closely we work each day: the teachers and students of the Tech 21 Academy.

When I was first offered a job teaching in Tech 21, I thought of it as job security; I now see that it was a chance to learn beside three master teachers in their respective content areas—Erica Beaton, Steve Vree, and Brooke Holt. It is humbling and inspiring to teach alongside those who are clearly my betters. I also don't know what I would do without our Tech 21 kids—I love you guys. We really are a family and a team. Erica, you especially were a dear encouragement to me when my blog was a tiny baby and you shared it in your many spheres, and also with your reminders that "done is better than perfect."

When I first began writing for teachers, it was for a self-started blog on an issue I wanted to learn about: the Common Core. Over the course of a hundred posts and countless more interactions, I have benefitted immeasurably from the community that has grown around a "non–freaked out approach" to the Common Core. Without you all, I would never have been motivated to keep on writing the blog posts that would eventually evolve into this book. Also, I'd be remiss not to mention that, when this started as a PDF ebook on the blog, Heather Bunker's cover design was instrumental in convincing folks to spend a dollar on it.

Along the journey of growing into a teacher-author, I was blessed to know two kind masters. I thank Jerry Graff, author of books with more than a million copies in print, who began a generous and rich email correspondence with me in September 2012. It's an understatement to say that you humble me. Similarly, I appreciate Jim Burke, who, like Jerry, initiated a bountiful, unsolicited correspondence through email almost a year ago. These juggernauts of the edu-writing world are heroes to me; if they are Obi-Wan Kenobi, I am a sprocket in R2-D2's head.

At the time that I was first contacted by Jossey-Bass about this book, I was being heavily influenced by the kind people at Staff Development for Educators, most notably Lisa Bingen, who has since become a dear friend, adviser, and mentor; Tom Schiele, who was and always will be my first editor; and Noële Faccidomo, who believed in me as a speaker far before I believed in myself. Lisa, you are far too gracious to me; Noële, you are far too kind to me; and Tom, I owe you a complex IPA the next time we meet.

When Jossey-Bass did contact me, it was through the kind and visionary Kate Bradford, my acquisitions editor, who somehow saw potential in the self-published ebook this book began as. Kate, thank you for taking a chance on me—it has made a great difference in my life. After Kate, the book went into the kind, able hands of Robin Lloyd, my production editor; Tracy Gallagher and Lily Miller, Robin's assistants; Francie Jones, my copyeditor (your eye is a work of wonder; all of my blog readers know how badly I need you, Francie); and Diane Turso, my proofreader (the same is true for you, Diane). Thank you all.

Finally (I know, right?), I dedicate this book to the two most influential people in my life: Crystal Stuart and Jesus of Nazareth. I can't escape the influence of either of you; you each call me to higher and higher ground; with every day, I fall more in love with both of you; when I die, I will look back and owe the most to the two of you, at the very least because you both put up with so much more from me than I deserve. I love you desperately, and in you I want for nothing.

ABOUT THE AUTHOR

Dave Stuart Jr. has taught in public schools for eight years; he currently teaches English and world history at Cedar Springs High School in Cedar Springs, Michigan. This is Dave's debut book, and it all began with the decision to start a little teacher blog in May 2012 called *Teaching the Core*. That blog has grown into a movement of over ten thousand monthly readers who refuse to freak out about the Common Core. In addition to teaching high school students, Dave enjoys his roles as an adjunct professor at Aquinas College and an educational consultant who travels around the country speaking to teachers. He holds a bachelor of arts in education and English from the University of Michigan and a master of education in curriculum and instruction from the American College of Education.

INTRODUCTION

AN EPIC JOURNEY BECKONS

Every great story pits a protagonist against overwhelming odds, and yet, through a combination of the protagonist's continued focus on the end goal and the help of various guides along the way, the grand journey ends in triumph. Despite the opposition of immortals, Odysseus returns to Ithaca; beneath the very eye of evil, Frodo destroys the one ring; regardless of the great power of the Sith, the Skywalkers bring balance to the Force. None of the epic heroes are perfect—many of the failures that punctuate their quests are caused by their own character flaws—and yet we cannot help but admire them, if for nothing else than their unquenchable desire to see the thing through.

Maybe it's the nerd in me, but whenever I stand back and take a wide perspective of the Common Core State Standards (CCSS) and the hubbub around them, I can't help but see the epic journey they invite us into. In this quest, you—whether you're a teacher, a parent, an administrator, or a policymaker—are the protagonist. The quest is absurdly large, as you seek to do nothing less than make sense of how to help students become people who flourish in the long term in a rapidly changing twenty-first century. Before the CCSS entered the scene, the conversations around this quest were varied, scattered, and isolated; now that forty-five states have adopted the standards, the conversation, with all of its passion and energy, has gained a widely shared focal point.

The CCSS, despite all the hoopla, are not the metaphorical equivalent of the evil Sauron or Sith—rather, they are simply a set of literacy skills that seek to describe what it means to be ready to succeed in college and in most careers. In fact, the CCSS do not even attempt to say *how* we should help students achieve mastery of these skills—they simply claim that these are the skills that matter most. To continue our metaphor, they are a destination for our quest. This book, then, is all about clearly understanding what that destination is.

A SWORD FOR YOUR QUEST

This book exists as a small aid to assist you with two particular obstacles on your journey. First, there is too much freaking out happening around the CCSS, and I hope to help you avoid drifting into anxiety. Education in the United States may need many things, but one of those things probably isn't more reasons to freak out. I think that, for every person out there who is eager to start a protest movement or launch a vitriolic website against the latest reform, there are those of us who simply want the information needed to do good work. And so at the heart of this book is a desire to allow you, whether you hold a stake in American education through being an educator or a parent or a policymaker, to see what the Common Core literacy standards actually say.

I want to be crystal clear here: this book aims to lessen the Common Core freak out through focusing on the Common Core, and that means I won't dwell on the big-budget, next-generation standardized tests that aim

to assess the skills in the CCSS. If you are searching for tips on how to increase student performance on the tests under development by the Smarter Balanced Assessment Consortium (SBAC) or Partnership for Assessment of Readiness for College and Careers (PARCC), this isn't your book. I have abandoned many ill-conceived notions that I brought with me into the profession of teaching, but one that I have held on to is that focusing on standardized tests won't do my students or me much good—this is especially true, it seems, with tests as new as those of the SBAC and PARCC groups. And so, to help you avoid freaking out about the Common Core, I'm going to strongly encourage you to focus on the standards themselves rather than on the tests designed to assess them. To revisit our quest metaphor, the tests are things we'll pass by on our way to the ultimate goal, but they are not the goal itself.

The second reason this book exists is to eradicate misinformation about the standards. In this book, we will simply read the anchor standards together, unpacking what they say and striving to remain as open minded as we can. I, like David Conley, "am neither an unqualified cheerleader for nor a harsh critic of the Common Core" (2014, p. 140). I seek to approach the standards pragmatically, and I see in these standards a chance to further promote long-term flourishing for students. It seems much more efficient, to me, to use the standards as an opportunity for growth rather than as a battle to die in. Essentially, my stance mirrors that of the eloquent Sarah Fine (2010, pp. 18–19), who wrote that

> what we need is to infuse the work around the common core [*sic*] with an element of visionary thinking. The standards themselves do not confine teaching to the realm of the scripted or the undemocratic, but without serious reflection and rethinking, they will. The balance depends on our collective ability to come to terms with the standards and to use them as an opportunity for reflection and growth.

In other words, I am of the ilk that sees in the Common Core both an opportunity and a danger, depending on how well educators and stakeholders come together around and use them.

In addition to the lack of bias I seek to bring to this book's treatment of the standards, I also write from the perspective of a regular, full-time secondary educator for whom the daily rigors of teaching make it impossible to venture too far into Sounds-Nice-but-It-Sure-Isn't-Practical Land. As a result, I seek in this book to get past the controversy and mythology and fear surrounding the standards by simply reading them at their broadest level: the level of the 32 anchor standards. I've found this to be an effective means of moving toward alleviating fears. It also aligns with my greater goal of helping teachers and stakeholders acquire a working knowledge of the aims of these standards— knowledge that can be leveraged to bring sanity back to the Common Core conversation and to the task of planning lessons that will influence and empower kids to dominate life in the long term.

THIS BOOK IS LIKE A TACO

Allow me to explain how this book is laid out. Part I is like a taco shell, containing the book's contents by focusing on the central, burning question of the CCSS (Chapter 1) and why that matters for our reading of the anchor standards (Chapter 2). Most people don't start with the overall aim of the standards, and as a result they get all worked up and overwhelmed when they read the specific standards. Reading the CCSS without a clear understanding of the whole is akin to trying to pick up a taco without a shell. It's inefficient at best, and it can mess up your pants at worst.

The remaining parts of the book—the fixin's, if you will—explore every one of the 32 anchor standards, unpacking the handful of skills present in each. For the sake of consistency, my treatment of every anchor standard numbers the skills as it unpacks them, and each of the four strands—reading, writing, speaking and listening, and language—begins with a simple overview. Also, in the appendix you'll find all of the 32 anchors contained on a two-page spread to help you quickly reference the list in its entirety.

As I explore each anchor standard, I'll share examples of how the target skill might look when approached in the secondary classroom. These examples, as you'll quickly surmise, come not from my imagination but from actual classrooms with real kids in them. The classroom most prominently drawn from is mine, where I teach freshman English and social studies; the other examples are drawn from the classrooms of my colleagues at Cedar Springs High School. The purpose of sharing these examples is to put flesh on the anchor standards. I do this for illustrative purposes and to generate thinking in the reader, with the clear caveat that no one in my school—most especially me—has it all figured out.

At the end of each anchor standard, I include a section titled "Why Is This Important?" I think this is one of the best questions my students ask, and I agree with Douglas Fisher (2014) that "a huge part of my paycheck comes because I have to figure out...how to make my content interesting and relevant for students." In other words, I want to help students learn not just how to do a thing, but why it's worth doing. I do this in pursuit of helping my students *own* their learning, because

no single factor may be more important to student success than the degree to which students take ownership of their learning...Not only does this key learning skill result in improved achievement, it is a more efficient and cost-effective way to manage the learning process. (Conley, 2014, p. 73)

Helping students own their learning, Common Core or otherwise, is one of those rare win-win situations in education, and so I use the "Why Is This Important?" sections to share some of the ways in which I explain the importance of these skills to my students.

A FINAL NOTE BEFORE DIVING IN

If at any point while you're reading this guide you have questions, please don't hesitate to contact me or to join the conversations happening at *Teaching the Core* (www.teachingthecore.com). With each passing month, that blog continues to grow into a community of sharp, committed educators who are determined to make the Common Core into a "win" for students and teachers. If you'd like to connect with me, I'm most easily reached through www .teachingthecore.com/contact-dave or https://twitter.com/davestuartjr. If you'd like to connect with a member of the *Teaching the Core* community, simply comment on any one of the posts on the blog.

Even if you don't have any questions, I'd love for you to come by and say hello!

PART I

Foundations

WHAT IS THE CENTRAL, BURNING QUESTION OF THE COMMON CORE STATE STANDARDS?

CHAPTER

1

I teach a secondary education methods class at a local college, and one of the first things I tell my undergrads is that, as a class, we will be a group of people driven by burning questions: big, complex, meaningful questions that we constantly find ourselves working on through our reading, writing, and conversations with others. I stress our cultivation of burning questions because, at the very outset of our semester together, I want my pre-service teachers to think less in terms of what assignments are due and more in terms of who they will be as teachers.

I desire this for them because burning questions spur us on. They make us work long after the contract says we can go home; they keep a notepad on our nightstand. They help us orient our mind to teaching as a calling, as a lifelong pursuit, rather than as a job or a means of gaining a pension. They are a secret strand that unites rising stars and established gurus in every field; they add a spark to the best writing we read, and they tend to create interesting lives.

But unless these questions have one central question to which they are subordinate, they can actually lead to a variety of pathologies, including this book's nemesis: the freak out.

So stop for a moment and consider this question:

> If you had to create a single, central, driving question that spurs on all of your most fulfilling and intriguing work as a teacher, what would it be?

My central, burning question, which took years to land on but has held up for years more, is simply this: How do I most effectively promote the long-term flourishing of my students? When I've got my head on straight, this question guides every decision I make in the classroom, and its answer trumps my opinions, philosophies, emotions, and ego. It's taken me years to even formulate this question, but I find that it's the only one broad enough to include all of my students and deep enough to challenge me year after year.

The reason I bring this up is that the easiest way for you to understand me as a teacher is for you to know my central, burning question. But more to the point of this book, the easiest way for you likewise to understand the Common Core is to grasp the central, burning question the standards aim to answer:

> What literacy skills does a high school graduate need to have to be college and career ready?

That's it. Not too wild of a question, right?

The Common Core State Standards (CCSS) answer this question with the 32 anchor standards. In all, there are 10 anchors in reading, 10 in writing, 6 in speaking and listening, and 6 in language. The simplest way to envision these is as a list of 32 literacy skills that college- and career-ready people possess. It's interesting to note that the CCSS lay responsibility for the reading and writing standards at the feet of not just English language arts (ELA) teachers but also teachers of history, social studies, science, and technical subjects. This is *not* to say that these non-ELA subjects should be reduced to mere literacy classes—as we'll discuss in the next chapter, a content-rich curriculum is critical for college and career readiness, according to the CCSS—but rather that literacy skills should be taught and developed in all the disciplines.

WHAT'S AN ANCHOR STANDARD?

When I first sat down to begin learning what the CCSS entailed, I had a hard time determining how to organize the task. After all, it's a sixty-six-page document with an eighteen-word title[1]—how

---

1. The title, in full, is *Common Core State Standards for English Language Arts and Literacy in History/Social Studies, Science, and Technical Subjects.* Though the standards are available in an online format at www .corestandards.org, throughout this book I will be citing from the actual standards document, which is available for download as a free PDF file at www.corestandards.org/wp-content/uploads/ELA _Standards.pdf.

do you turn that into something manageable, searchable, teachable, and perhaps even embraceable?

The key is the anchor standards. Remember how the CCSS were made to describe what a college- and career-ready person needs to be able to do? Anchor standards are simply descriptions of college and career readiness skills. Thus, there are ten descriptions of what a college- and career-ready person can do in reading, ten of what she can do in writing, six of what he can do in speaking and listening, and six of what she can do in language.

WHY CALL THEM "ANCHORS"?

Because the CCSS are all about determining what a college- and career-ready person can do, college and career readiness skills are what the CCSS want every grade level to be "anchored" to. Postsecondary life is the bedrock the CCSS authors have planted the anchor in, hoping to keep the ship steadily pulling in to a bright shore along the rope of a K–12 education (see Figure 1.1).

Put another way, the anchor standards are general descriptions of what a K–12 education aims at under the CCSS. Whether you teach kindergarten

or twelfth grade, the anchor standards are the ultimate destination.

WHY NOT JUST USE THE GRADE-SPECIFIC STANDARDS?

Because K–12 schooling is complex, the CCSS document gets increasingly complicated once you dive deeper than the anchor standards. For example, from kindergarten through grade 5, the anchor standards in reading are broken into the categories of literature, informational texts, and foundational skills. From grades 6 through 12, however, those same reading anchor standards are broken into the categories of ELA and "literacy in history/social studies, science, and technical subjects." All of this complexity is simply for the purpose of translating the broad anchor standards into specific, appropriate, end-of-grade expectations.

Okay, so let's not go there in this book. This is meant to guide you into starting with the CCSS, not to bury you (and me) in the specifics. But when you are ready to delve into the grade-specific standards, I recommend the user-friendly resource I use: Jim Burke's *The Common Core Companion* (2013). Jim is a prolific teacher-author who has remained in the public

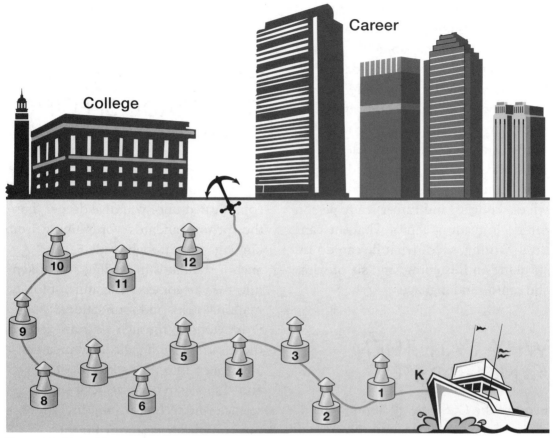

Figure 1.1 A Visual Representation of the Anchor Standards

school classroom for decades and still teaches there today; I cannot laud his work, or his Common Core resource, enough.

In this book, we'll focus on the anchor standards. Think about it: the anchor standards represent the fundamental skills that the CCSS believe students need to have when they graduate from our public schools. They are general enough to allow for the entre-preneurial aspects of being a teaching professional (that is, they give us room to play), but they are also rigorous (which, I have found, kids can learn to appreciate), and they are aligned with what the majority of colleges and workplaces expect students to be able to do. These anchors are what can keep our kids from floating away sometime between their entry into kindergarten and the fateful tassel flip.

THE COMMON CORE'S BROADEST ANSWER TO ITS CENTRAL, BURNING QUESTION

Before we jump into the anchor standards, which give more specific answers to the central question of the Common Core State Standards (CCSS), let's look at a broad overview of college and career readiness that the authors of the CCSS included on page 7 of the introductory matter of the standards (National Governors Association Center for Best Practices [NGA] & Council of Chief State School Officers [CCSSO], 2010). This is an important page for any teacher, parent, or other stakeholder, because if you don't agree that a college- and career-ready person can do these things, you'll be likely to disagree with some or all of the rest of the document.

When determining whether I agreed with these standards initially, I came to them with my aforementioned central, burning question in mind. I wondered: *Will the college- and career-ready person described by the CCSS be someone likely to flourish after graduation?* To answer that, I examined the broad overview of college and career readiness provided in the introductory matter of the CCSS, which explains that a college- and career-ready person can do the following (NGA & CCSSO, 2010, p. 7):

1. "Demonstrate independence"

2. "Build strong content knowledge"

3. "Respond to…audience, task, purpose, and discipline"

4. "Comprehend as well as critique"

5. "Value evidence"

6. "Use technology…strategically and capably"

7. "Come to understand other perspectives and cultures"

Let's look at each of these in more detail.

DEMONSTRATE INDEPENDENCE

College- and career-ready people can, without having their hand held by a teacher, comprehend a diverse array of complex texts; and, using these texts, they are able to make sensible arguments and communicate complicated information. In other words, if you hand a college- and career-ready person an inorganic chemistry textbook or a training manual, she is not going to look from it to you with lamblike eyes.

Likewise, when listening to a speaker, this person is able to pick up on main points, identify where she is confused, request clarification, ask relevant questions, and competently and thoughtfully engage in a group discussion. Whether they're sitting in an Intro to Literature discussion group or listening to a colleague present the past quarter's numbers, college- and career-ready folks can hold their own.

Furthermore, they are independently able to use standard English in befitting situations, and they have access to a wide vocabulary. They probably text in what Great-Grandma would assume is a different language, but when the task, purpose, or audience calls for it, college- and career-ready people know how to communicate in the kind of English used by those in power.

BUILD STRONG CONTENT KNOWLEDGE

Some have heard that the CCSS aim to destroy content—students will now only learn skills, and they won't be required to gain any knowledge. This is an especially dangerous and entirely baseless myth. As you see here and as you'll see when reading the anchor standards themselves, Common Core implementation approaches that seek to diminish content knowledge are egregiously misinterpreting the aim of the standards and are likely to fail at the expense of our students.

According to the introduction to the standards, college- and career-ready people are lifelong knowledge builders, and this knowledge is built on a robust K–12 foundation. They build knowledge at both broad and discipline-specific levels by engaging with "high-quality works" (NGA & CCSSO, 2010, p. 7). Essentially, these people enjoy accumulating knowledge, thanks to their participation in a coherent, content-rich K–12 curriculum. Though the CCSS intentionally avoid dictating what this content should be, they are not shy about insisting that it should be rich and increasingly complex as the grades progress.

RESPOND TO TASK, AUDIENCE, PURPOSE, AND DISCIPLINE

As mentioned earlier, college- and career-ready people understand that effective communicators adapt to their context. If they're trying to gain the boss's support for an idea, they will communicate one way, but if they are trying to articulate insights from an experiment, they will communicate another way. They know that written and spoken conventions vary based on a variety of factors, and that a smiley face emoticon is not appropriate for an argumentative essay. ☺ In short, college- and career-ready people recognize the communicative demands of a given situation.

COMPREHEND AS WELL AS CRITIQUE

Most people are quick to comprehend or quick to critique; few do both. For example, my students and I were reading *Animal Farm* (Orwell, 1945) one time, and we were discussing the use of propaganda. I asked students to conduct Google searches for various types of propaganda, and, though what they found ranged from hilarious to haunting, I was most taken aback by a proud student displaying a faux political campaign poster on which President Barack Obama's head, chin tilted high, was positioned over a single, bold-print word: "SNOB."

After capturing and silencing the doomsaying monkeys inside of my head that see such sardonic name-calling toward the executive branch as a sign of America's end times, I was able to look at this "text" in terms of college and career readiness.

According to the CCSS, students who are college and career ready would be able to both comprehend and critique this image. They are open minded, yet discerning; they "work diligently to understand precisely what an author or speaker is saying, but they also question an author's or speaker's assumptions and premises and assess the veracity of claims and the soundness of reasoning" (NGA & CCSSO, 2010, p. 7).

And so, in this case, a college- and career-ready person would understand what the poster was referring to (claims that President Obama is an elitist), yet he could also question where these claims come from. A college- and career-ready person would be able to do this no matter which side of the political spectrum she personally agreed with, and, if she had questions (for example, Where do claims of President Obama's elitism originate?), she would have either the gumption to look them up or the honesty to say that she wasn't sure about the answers.

VALUE EVIDENCE

When sharing their interpretations of a movie, a newspaper, an all-company email, or a syllabus, college- and career-ready people cite specific evidence as a habit of mind. "No, Captain America wasn't a perfect hero," one of my students once said. "After all, he kissed that random girl while the girl he actually loved watched. Fail." At first I ignored the comment as one of the many random data points in the day of a teacher; yet after a minute I found myself sharing this student's statement with the entire class as a down-to-earth example of the use of textual evidence, explaining that, in this case, the "text" was a movie.

CLAIM: Captain America is not a perfect hero.
EVIDENCE: He kissed the random girl.

In addition, college- and career-ready people make their reasoning clear to their reader or listener. In other words, they don't just do what I call "quote bombing"—where you drop in a quote that backs up your argument without any explanation of how it does so—instead making clear what a given piece of evidence is being used for.

USE TECHNOLOGY STRATEGICALLY AND CAPABLY

College- and career-ready people have a clear idea of the strengths and limitations of technology. They use Wikipedia for developing background knowledge,[1] not for proving a point in an argument. They appreciate the spell-checker, but they know that it doesn't catch homonyms; they install extensions in their Web browser that make definitions of

---

1. For a fascinating treatment of the proper academic uses of Wikipedia, see Wikipedia's own http://en.wikipedia.org/wiki/Wikipedia:Academic_use.

difficult words a double-click away, but they know that words have nuances and multiple meanings; they habitually Google a question if they have one, and they try various ways of posing the question if they don't quickly find the information they're looking for. In other words, a college- and career-ready person sees technology as a tool, not as a shiny object or an omniscient benefactor.

COME TO UNDERSTAND OTHER PERSPECTIVES AND CULTURES

Finally, college- and career-ready students recognize that generalizations about peoples, places, tribes, and races are always inaccurate. There is no one thing that all white people do. There is no one attitude that all Muslims have. There is no one temperament of all black people.

Human beings are perhaps unquantifiably complex, especially in groups, and rather than fear this truth or generalize it away, college- and career-ready people actively seek to understand perspectives and cultures different from their own. This does not necessitate swallowing a postmodern, relativistic view of the world; it just means that the college- and career-ready person is on a quest for understanding.

A NOTE FROM DAVE

Well done! You've made it through the introductory content of this book. I hope you now feel comfortable with terms like "CCSS," "college and career ready," and "anchor standards." Next, we'll begin this book's main work, which is looking at the anchor standards themselves. Before we do that, though, I should tell you that the notation for a CCSS anchor standard looks like this: R.CCR.1. In this case, "R" stands for "reading"; "CCR" stands for "college and career readiness" (in other words, it's like it's saying, "This is an anchor standard"); and "1" indicates that this is the 1st standard in the reading anchor standards.

Also, although this book is focused on the anchor standards, I will occasionally reference grade-level standards for the sake of clarifying what a given anchor standard is getting at. When I do this, you'll see notations like this: L.3.2. In this case, "L" stands for "language"; "3" stands for "grade 3"; and "2" indicates that this is the 2nd standard in the language standards. In other words, it describes the skills a third grader should have to be on pace for college and career readiness in the second language anchor standard.

PART II

The Anchor Standards in Reading

ARE YOU HUNGRY FOR SOME INCREASED READING ANCHOR STANDARD COMPREHENSION? I totally am. We have a simple, overarching question to keep in mind while going over these ten anchor standards: What do the Common Core State Standards say a college- and career-ready reader should be able to do?

HOW ARE THE ANCHOR STANDARDS IN READING ORGANIZED?

The 10 anchor standards in reading are broken up into 4 groups:

1. Key Ideas and Details (R.CCR.1–3)

2. Craft and Structure (R.CCR.4–6)

3. Integration of Knowledge and Ideas (R.CCR.7–9)

4. Range and Level of Text Complexity (R.CCR.10)

Or, in everyday human terms, these anchor standards are dedicated to answering these questions:

1. What does the text say? What does it not say? What does it mean? How can you prove it?

2. How does the author use language to communicate? How is the text organized? Who wrote this, and how and why does that matter?

3. How does this text connect with other sources? Does it measure up? Is it valid?

4. How do you handle a broad range of high-quality texts?

Onward.

The 1st college and career readiness anchor standard within the reading strand of the Common Core State Standards (CCSS) reads as follows:

> Read closely to determine what the text says explicitly and to make logical inferences from it; cite specific textual evidence when writing or speaking to support conclusions drawn from the text.

I appreciate that the CCSS reading and writing strands each limit themselves to 10 anchor standards. Ten is a clean number; it's manageable. That being said, as you can see from the text of R.CCR.1, each anchor standard can contain multiple skills—that's why the grade-specific Common Core literacy standards have many subbullets. Our focus, however, is on the college and career readiness benchmarks laid out in each anchor standard. So what, then, must a college- and career-ready person be able to do, according to the first reading anchor?

READ CLOSELY

Close reading is the core of this anchor standard, and, if you'll allow me to treat what others have dedicated books to in a single sentence, it is simply what we do when we're trying to figure out a particular, manageable part of a complex text. "Figuring it out" can mean any of dozens of things, many of which are explored in the other reading anchor standards. This particular anchor focuses on two biggies: figuring out (1) what a text actually says and (2) what it says without directly saying it. It then deals with the need to figure things out logically rather than haphazardly.

Before going into those elements of this anchor standard, it's worth noting that, at the time of this writing, "close reading" is a leading contender for buzzword of the year, and many educators are already tiring of its use. Although there is plenty of nuance to what it means to intensely, attentively engage with a text, I do think it can be a bit overwhelming to obsess over what it means to read closely. Toward that end, just remember that our goal here isn't to invent hundreds of close reading lessons, but rather to produce graduates who habitually and unconsciously read portions of texts closely on an as-needed basis.

Across the disciplines, the fastest and most effective way to help students get to the place of automatic close reading is by giving them access to loads of intriguing and diverse texts, and then modeling for them the act of examining sections of the readings closely. In my world history classroom, this means that, in any given week, my students will read some or all of the following: primary source documents (ranging from declarations to paintings to sculptures); pages from informational texts (including our textbook); recently published articles; and video clips (for example, John Green's fast-paced, information-rich, humor-laden, argumentative *Crash Course World History* video series on YouTube, found at www.youtube.com/user/crashcourse).

The key to getting students to own close reading tasks is to make our classrooms places where reading, writing, and speaking about ideas and questions are standard procedure—and where modeling these activities for students is our standard instructional practice. When assigning students a text, give a purpose for reading the text or have students develop one, and then teach students how to strategically read the text in a manner that helps them succeed at the purpose.

For example, it's become commonplace to equate close reading with simply annotating a text. But when annotation is used as a way to encourage slowing down and working through a text attentively, it's critical that students know the purpose for their reading and annotate accordingly. In other words, annotation serves an end in close reading—it is not an end in itself.

I remember a student from several years ago, Caleb, who realized the strategic nature of worthwhile annotation for the first time. He normally struggled with the "article of the week" (Gallagher, 2009, p. 47) assignment in my world history class, but about midway through the year he turned in an exemplary written response to the week's article. When I approached him about the sudden improvement in his work, he said that, when it came time to respond to the article in writing, he simply went back to his annotations—which, in this case, he had used to mark places where he'd had a genuine response to the argument the article's author was making. As a result, there was a fluid transition between his close reading of the article and his written response to it. It's also worth noting that Caleb made a valuable contribution to the next day's discussion as well.

The key, then, is not simply making our kids mark up texts arbitrarily, but rather having them do so strategically.

DETERMINE LITERAL, EXPLICIT MEANING

The literal meaning of a text answers the question, What does it say? Obviously, if we can't figure this out, we're not going to do very well at going deeper with questions like, What does it mean? or Why does it matter? Across the disciplines, teachers are helping students with this step by modeling basic comprehension strategies via think-aloud reading.[1] For teachers unfamiliar with reading instruction, the goal of think-aloud reading is simply to read a portion of a passage aloud while also speaking aloud some of the things we think—questions or comments or strategies we use as readers. Before allowing students to tackle a text on their own, we teachers, the best readers in the room, are wise to read aloud for them with some of our thinking, which reveals for our students the invisible mental processes that go on when we're discovering what a text says for the first time.

MAKE LOGICAL INFERENCES

If I tell you that every time I speak in public my throat gets dry and I begin swallowing compulsively, you can gather that I experience nervousness when talking to groups of people. I haven't explicitly told you that, but you've learned it from what I've said nonetheless. Inference is the art of figuring out what a text is saying without saying it. If our inferences are logical, they are based on what the text clearly says. Thus, the skill of inferring builds on the skill of figuring out what a text says outright.

---

1. See Mike Schmoker's short and sweet treatment of "modeling higher-order reading" (2011, pp. 79–81).

In *Deeper Reading*, Kelly Gallagher (2004) shares the following passage he uses to ease students into the concept of inference. While reading it, Gallagher asks his students to guess where the narrator is sitting:

> I can't believe I have been sitting here among all these sick people for over an hour waiting for them to call my name. Why do they overschedule so many patients? I hope I am called next, for I don't know how much longer I can tolerate this sore throat. (p. 81)

Even though the passage doesn't literally say, "I am sitting in the doctor's office," it gives plenty of clues telling us as much.

The problem with teaching inference is, again, that it's often an unconscious skill—no one says, "All right, I'm going to infer that the narrator is sitting in an emergency room"; rather, our brain simply deduces that, based on the evidence. This process only breaks down when we are faced with texts complex enough to strain our current abilities. Thus, to help students gain the ability to make inferences, a solid teaching strategy is modeling inferential thinking via think-aloud reading. This gives students an explicit model for working through a text logically and strategically.

SUPPORT CONCLUSIONS WITH TEXTUAL EVIDENCE

A core skill woven through the anchor standards is the ability to support one's thinking with textual evidence. Every claim or insight during a discussion around a text should be undergirded with support from the text. When I first ask students to do this, it's clunky—there's no other way to put it. They say things during discussion like "I got that from page 22 of the article" after making statements. And although it's my job to model for them how to cite textual evidence in a smooth manner, they simply won't get good at it if I don't give them an abundance of opportunities to do it. And so, whether we're debating an issue informed by texts, writing academic papers, or simply having an impromptu discussion, building habitual evidence users is as simple as asking my students, "From what did you draw that conclusion?" or "Where does the text say that?" or "What in the text, specifically, backs up your argument?"

The aim here is not to badger kids, just as the aim in this anchor standard isn't to butcher the joyful task of reading. Instead, it's about making sure they know not just *that* they are right, but *why* they are right.

WHY IS THIS IMPORTANT?

First of all, this anchor standard includes the ability to understand what a text says—basically, the ability to read. That's kind of a biggie.

Even more than this, what's at stake with R.CCR.1 is developing graduates who ground their opinions in evidence instead of graduates who find their opinions valuable simply because they exist. I am all for every person's having a right to his own two cents and the freedom to openly express them, but I want my students to know that our right to an opinion doesn't make our opinion valuable or respectable or, well, even right. When we read texts closely to research our opinions, when we can argue from research why a new product line will benefit the country, when we can support our political or religious doctrine with texts as well as our gut feelings, then I think we haven't just got a *right* to be heard—we actually *will* be.

2

The 2nd college and career readiness anchor standard within the reading strand of the CCSS reads as follows:

> Determine central ideas or themes of a text and analyze their development; summarize the key supporting details and ideas.

Here we see a natural progression from R.CCR.1, as basic comprehension deepens into the ability to figure out what a text is focused on, how it develops that focus, and how to quickly communicate that focus.

DECIDE ON WHAT'S CENTRAL

"Central ideas or themes" are what the text is mostly about. In other words, What, if you stripped away all superfluous details, would this text be about? If you had to limit this text's point or message to a sentence or a tweet, what would it say?

Deciding on what's central is perhaps easiest done with informational texts, as authors tend to make explicit what they are most trying to communicate through the use of statements, transitions, headings, captions, and other structural elements. Yet even when reading informational texts, many students still struggle with this decision. One method for helping them break through mental barriers is asking them to generate every possible thing the text *could* be mainly about, and then having them go through each possibility to see which is most thoroughly developed by the text (Burke, 2013).

In the historical disciplines, this ability becomes even more crucial. Take, for instance, a hypothetical textbook chapter on World War II. There may be illustrative details like photos of contemporary military technology or anecdotes from soldiers and civilians, and yet students who are prepared for college-level history coursework must be able to determine what such sections are meant to convey about the most significant aspects of World War II. I have students every year who can recite all kinds of facts about this war (thank you, History Channel), but rare is the student who can explain the significance of these facts from a broader historical perspective.

In science, this ability to determine central ideas is also critical. When I read about the detailed cellular or molecular processes involved in photosynthesis, for example, it's easy to become overwhelmed with the intricate minutiae involved. But if I can first go through a text gathering the big ideas—say, the major steps in photosynthesis—the information becomes much more manageable and I'm able to then go back in and reread for details.

Determining central themes in literature is often a more difficult task, because literary writing tends to be less explicit about the topics it explores through stories and stanzas.

Take, for example, David Huddle's "Only the Little Bone" (1986), a short story my students read each year. In the story, the narrator recounts anecdotes from his youth and from his adulthood, and he uses these stories to illustrate a trait—what he calls "flawed competence" (p. 212)—that he shares with his grandfather. For example, he describes a time that his grandfather built him crutches that didn't work quite right, and the time his grandfather helped him build a semifunctional basketball court. The story is mainly about this trait—how it shows itself in the narrator's family while he is growing up, and how it shows itself in him as an adult—but the student who isn't proficient in the skills of R.CCR.2 might say that the text is mainly about the narrator's life (too general) or about the time he built a basketball court with his grandpa (too specific).

PULL APART HOW THAT CENTRAL THING IS DEVELOPED

It's one thing to know what a text is mainly about; it's a greater thing to know how an author develops that central thing. Understanding how authors use details or reasoning to build a piece of writing's main thrust will allow us to read strategically and with greater comprehension, and, as a nice bonus, it will help us write better as well.

The photosynthesis text illustrates the clearest example of how the central idea is developed: the author describes the steps through which plants use sunlight to synthesize foods from carbon dioxide and water. In the World War II example, the author may be using participant anecdotes and diagrams of new weapons to illustrate the lasting psychological toll that modern weapons had on those involved. And in regard to the short story example, college- and career-ready students should be able to say that one reason why they know the story is about the narrator's discovery that he, too, has the family trait is that each anecdote contains reflection on the trait as it appeared in his relatives and appears in himself.

SUMMARIZE THE TEXT

Summarization is one of those not-very-sexy-but-pretty-darn-powerful abilities that college- and career-ready people possess. Yes, we must be able to come up with our own thoughts and develop our own arguments, and every teacher, after reading a set of student papers, has probably thought, at least once, something along the lines of, *If one more student summarizes X in these papers, I'm going to defenestrate a gerbil.* But the ability to succinctly, accurately, and

objectively explain what a text is mostly about while using key supporting details and ideas to back up one's explanation is a key skill for career and college literacy tasks.

Take, for example, the task of building an argument. Although many students (much to the chagrin of their future spouses and college professors) are taught that argumentation is about proving your point, one of the most popular college writing textbooks goes to great pains to teach students the critical importance of first establishing—through objective summarization and paraphrasing—what other people have said about an issue before launching into one's own opinion. This textbook—indicatively titled *They Say, I Say: The Moves That Matter in Academic Writing* and authored by two leading thinkers in the field, Gerald Graff and Cathy Birkenstein (2014)—turns out to be useful not just for developing the skill of being fair in one's arguments but also for simply being effective in arguing for one's position. Such powerful, conscientious argumentation is useful both in academia and in adult life in general.

WHY IS THIS IMPORTANT?

Essentially, the college- and career-ready person envisioned here is one able to accurately see and explain big ideas and the details that help communicate them. Whether reading a fellow employee's email to the team, a professor's assignment instructions, a procedural write-up, or a short story, college- and career-ready people habitually decide on the main points in a given text and can point to how they found them. In a world in which new information equivalent to the entire sum of information produced by mankind up until 2003 is currently created in less than two days (Siegler, 2010), the ability to quickly determine a text's central idea and summarize doesn't seem likely to decrease in importance.

The 3rd college and career readiness anchor standard within the reading strand of the CCSS reads as follows:

> Analyze how and why individuals, events, or ideas develop and interact over the course of a text.

The skills in this anchor can be split up into the central questions of how and why, and are best explained with a few examples.

HOW DO INDIVIDUALS, EVENTS, OR IDEAS DEVELOP AND INTERACT OVER THE COURSE OF A TEXT?

Okay, so there are actually lots of questions within this question. Because the development of ideas is covered pretty thoroughly in R.CCR.2, however, let's look at examples of how an individual and an event develop over the course of a text.

For the development of an individual, let's consider Okonkwo in Chinua Achebe's *Things Fall Apart* (1959). I choose Achebe's work for several reasons. First, my freshmen and I read it in world history class each winter. Second, it's a text exemplar on page 10 of the Common Core's Appendix B (National Governors Association Center for Best Practices [NGA] & Council of Chief State School Officers [CCSSO], 2010). Third, it takes care of the 6th Common Core reading standard, which, for grades 9 and 10, specifically calls for students to experience "a wide reading of world literature" (RL.9–10.6). And fourth, it's a haunting, thought-provoking book about the nature of masculinity and the distortions of imperialistic worldviews.

Analyzing Okonkwo's development over the course of the text is tricky because, at first glance, it appears that

Okonkwo changes little, beginning and ending the novel as a man driven by his fear of appearing weak. When students struggle with this task, it's helpful to remind them that when someone analyzes a character, she carefully examines that character's thoughts and actions to determine how those small pieces work together to create a complete (and, in the case of Okonkwo, complex) picture of who that character is. On further analysis, then, it's clear that Okonkwo does change throughout his life: at one point, his initial romance with Ekwefi gives us a glimpse of a younger, freer Okonkwo; after killing Ikemefuna, Okonkwo spends days in anguish, unable to eat because of what he has done; and so on.

Events are a bit different, but that core skill of analysis—examining smaller things to see how they come together to create a deeper understanding of the larger whole—is again the core intellectual skill. When considering the Enlightenment, for example, students might read excerpts from Montesquieu, Rousseau, Locke, Voltaire, Wollstonecraft, and Jefferson, seeking to determine which of these thinkers drew from their peers and which truly developed the core tenets of the Enlightenment that continue to be worked out in societies across the globe today.

WHY DO INDIVIDUALS, EVENTS, OR IDEAS DEVELOP AND INTERACT OVER THE COURSE OF A TEXT?

One of my colleagues (a math teacher named Chris Painter) is infamous among students for his perpetual use of probing questions. When students make a statement (for example, "The solution is 4"), he'll ask, "Why?" or he'll say, "Explain." When they answer, he'll simply repeat his question, and so on. Some of his students are initially annoyed at how much thinking they are forced to do in his class, but by the end of a course with him, they possess a deeper understanding of the principles that underlie the mathematical procedures they thought they understood but instead had simply memorized. Essentially, Painter doesn't just force them to look at the "what" and "how" of mathematics; he pushes them to grapple with the "why," much to their initial chagrin and lingering benefit.

Now, to apply this to R.CCR.3, let's say my freshman students are discussing why individuals develop, and we're reading *Things Fall Apart*. I could ask them what kind of an individual

Okonkwo is, and they might tell me, "Well, he's obsessed with being strong and successful."

"Why?"

"Um, because his dad was weak. He was a humiliation to Okonkwo."

"Okay, why?"

"Because Umuofian society values strength?"

"Was there a question mark at the end of that statement?"

"No. Umuofian society does value strength."

"Do you have specific evidence for that?" (By the way, simple questions like this help students make R.CCR.1 a habit.)

Going a bit deeper, R.CCR.3 is also getting at how authors use characters like Okonkwo to develop themes and advance plots. I'll sometimes ask my literature students whether they think a certain character or relationship or event develops a theme or simply moves the plot forward. With *Things Fall Apart*, I might ask, "Why does Achebe have Okonkwo grow close to Ikemefuna and then kill him?" or "What is the point of Okonkwo and Ezinma's odd father–daughter relationship?"

WHY IS THIS IMPORTANT?

At its core, this standard assumes college- and career-ready people will encounter a variety of complex texts in which authors write with intentionality. Analyzing individual characters or event sequences may seem like joy-killing work, but it ultimately builds a habitual, analytical approach to texts that, although valuable in and of itself, is transferable to the ability to analyze one's own life to piece together seemingly disparate experiences into useful, insightful lessons.

Notice how this set of skills builds on those in the previous standard. When a person is able to efficiently determine the central ideas of a piece of writing, he can then work to consider how and why the details interact and develop. This skill can result in profound insights into everything from gross profit reports to water cooler discussions, and the ability to produce such insights is impressive to professors and invaluable to employers.

The 4th college and career readiness anchor standard within the reading strand of the CCSS reads as follows:

> Interpret words and phrases as they are used in a text, including determining technical, connotative, and figurative meanings, and analyze how specific word choices shape meaning or tone.

Notice how R.CCR.2 dealt with central ideas, R.CCR.3 zoomed in a bit to explore the relationships between details, and now R.CCR.4 focuses still closer on the word level of texts.

INTERPRET WORDS AND PHRASES

When we read, our respective brains' "word meaning, or semantic, systems contribute every possible meaning of each word [we] read and incorporate the exact correct meaning for each word in its context" (Wolf, 2007, p. 8). Sounds intense, right? Actually, this work is subconscious until we're faced with texts that contain unfamiliar words and phrases. This anchor has us focus on several questions we grapple with when faced with situations our semantic system doesn't automatically resolve for us:

- What are the technical meanings of words and phrases in a text?

- What are the connotative and denotative meanings?

- What are the figurative meanings?

Before we treat each of these in turn, let's deal with an important word in this standard: "interpret." Interpretation is the act of explaining what someone says in a manner accessible to someone with less familiarity with the subject at hand (for example, when a child in elementary school seeks to interpret an adult's words for a toddler sibling). This standard thus envisions a person who can read a piece of writing and explain the use of words in a manner that would be accessible to someone with less understanding.

Technical Meanings

Let's begin with questions of technical meaning, which shouldn't be confused with denotative (or literal) meaning, which we'll discuss next. Technical words "would be [those] with specialized meanings specific to the subject being investigated, explained, or argued about; one example might be the distinctions made between political philosophies, such as libertarian and republican" (Burke, 2013, p. 28). Consider, as another example, the terms "supply" and "demand." In most contexts, these are simple terms; in economic texts, however, they have a much more significant, complex meaning. In other words, they have a technical meaning in the context of economics, and the ability to detect and interpret technical meanings when they're in play is part of what this anchor standard is getting at.

Connotative and Denotative Meanings

Although denotative meaning isn't explicitly mentioned in this anchor standard, I don't know of an easier way to teach connotation than through the use of its cousin denotation. Denotation, on the one hand, refers to the literal meaning of a word; if you search in the dictionary, you will find a word's denotative meanings. Connotation, on the other hand, has to do with the idea or feeling that a word invokes for a person; a dictionary may make occasional hints at connotation, but connotation is naturally a bit more subjective than denotation and therefore a bit harder to organize in reference format.

For instance, Hiroshima, denotatively, is a city in Japan. Connotatively, however, the word "Hiroshima" changes based on your personal perspective. At the same time, connotation is not entirely out of the author's control; there are ways an author can shape connotation for her readers. For example, consider these two sentences:

1. The megalomaniacal dictator dreamed of the day when his city, with its crimes against humanity, would merit inclusion in lists of places where the greatest evils of the past century had taken place: Auschwitz, Rwanda, North Korea, Hiroshima.

2. The *Enola Gay* flew the most important mission of World War II; because of its heroic mission to

Hiroshima, countless American and Japanese lives were saved.

In both sentences, the denotation of the word "Hiroshima" has not changed. But because sentence 1 lists Hiroshima with sites of horrible crimes against humanity whereas sentence 2 associates Hiroshima with words like "important," "heroic," and "lives saved," the authors have created starkly different connotations for the word. This is what we want students to be able to discern. For a given sentence, we can ask:

- What does this word literally mean? What is its denotation?
- What feelings and ideas does this word evoke? What is its connotation?
- How does the author use the words around our target word to shape its connotation?

Figurative Meanings

In addition, college- and career-ready people need to understand when a text is speaking figuratively, and whenever someone uses the phrase "figurative language," my mind responds with Pavlovian precision, instantly conjuring the cover of Ray Bradbury's *Fahrenheit 451* (1953). My freshman literature students read this book each year, and I know of no other text with more figurative language per square inch. Personally, I'm not a fan of what I view as Bradbury's overuse of similes and metaphors in *Fahrenheit*, but the book is perfect for cementing in my students' minds what figurative language is and how one interprets it.

Figurative language is present, simply, when an author literally says one thing but means something else. So for example, on the first page of *Fahrenheit*—which, by the way, is a text exemplar in Appendix B for grades 9 and 10 (NGA & CCSSO, 2010, p. 10)—we read about a "great python spitting its venomous kerosene upon the world" (Bradbury, 1953, p. 1). If a student is college and career ready according to R.CCR.4, he will be able to figure out while reading the passage that Bradbury is talking about a fire hose, not a snake, and that it's spitting regular kerosene on a house, not on the entire world.

They'll also be able to see how this choice of figurative language begins to develop a sinister tone in the book—and to discuss that, let's move on.

ANALYZE WORD CHOICE

This final part of R.CCR.4 could be illustrated with our previous discussion of the word "Hiroshima" or Bradbury's use of figurative language, but let's look at another example.

Consider Rudyard Kipling's poem "The White Man's Burden" (1899), which I use to introduce students to ideas we explore in our study of *Things Fall Apart* (Achebe, 1959). When we read this poem, the main thing I want students to detect is Kipling's tone when he refers to nonwhite colonial subjects. When discussing tone, I tell students to think of tone of voice. I give them several exaggerated examples of how an adult's tone can be condescending or encouraging or inspiring or insulting. I ask them how I achieve each of those tones in my demonstration, and though at first they may mention that it's the way in which I spoke, they'll quickly surmise that it also had to do with the words I chose to use.

Kipling's poem is a challenge for my freshman students, so I begin our work with it by reading it aloud as they follow along. After I finish our initial reading, I ask students to quickly write down their first reactions to specific lines in the poem (I ask, "Where were you surprised or confused?"), and then I have them talk to a partner about a specific line that they responded to. (In addition to giving them another way in which to process the poem, this gives them practice with clear, evidence-based communication, which W.CCR.9 and

SL.CCR.4 call for.) Having now entered the poem through these activities, we are ready to begin drilling down into how specific word choices shape tone and meaning.

Just as in my exaggerated examples of adult tones of voice, a text's tone often communicates the author's attitude toward his subject. To help my students detect Kipling's attitude toward the white man's "burden," in our next reading I ask students to underline every word that Kipling uses to refer to the colonial subjects his poem focuses on. After this second reading, we quickly create a class list of these words, which include

- Burden (lines 1, 9, 17 . . .)
- Captive's (line 4)
- Fluttered folk (line 6)
- Wild (line 6)
- New-caught (line 7)
- Sullen peoples (line 7)
- Half-devil (line 8)
- Half-child (line 8)

Once we complete our list, it's time for discussion of the following questions, in table groups and as a class:

- Taken together, what do these word choices indicate about Kipling's attitude toward colonial subjects?

How do they accumulate into a loud and clear message?

- What adjectives would you use to describe Kipling's tone toward colonial subjects?

- If such a poem were written about you and a group you belong to, how might you respond?

Once I feel that this discussion has prepared us to begin considering Achebe's motivations in writing *Things Fall Apart*, I ask students to write how Kipling's word choice shapes his tone. In writing this response, they are expected to cite textual evidence (R.CCR.1). I am seeking constantly to weave the standards together into a cohesive set of habits that literate people instinctively bring to any communicative act.

WHY IS THIS IMPORTANT?

Tasks around word meaning and word choice can quickly become irrelevant to our students if these are reduced to worksheets and busywork. And yet, if we do not develop the ability to think deeply about the nuances and power of word choice, a number of blunders await us. Think, for example, of the email battles almost all of us have experienced at least once. So often, heated email exchanges begin simply because of ill-considered word choices that intentionally or unintentionally create an offensive tone. These exchanges only get hotter when the participants begin to say, "I never wrote that you are an idiot," even though they actually did communicate disdain through the cumulative effect of their choice of words and the connotative meanings attached to them. Sometimes these exchanges simply create hurt feelings—no small matter to a person who wants to live a flourishing life. But often they can lead to much worse consequences, like severed relationships or terminated employment.

To avoid these problems, college- and career-ready individuals write beautifully clear emails, taking pains to "overcommunicate" their tone. Such people find that they are able to communicate in such a way that what they convey—electronically or otherwise—is received in the manner intended: a seemingly simple, yet profoundly powerful ability.

R.CCR. 5

The 5th college and career readiness anchor standard within the reading strand of the CCSS reads as follows:

Analyze the structure of texts, including how specific sentences, paragraphs, and larger portions of the text (e.g., a section, chapter, scene, or stanza) relate to each other and the whole.

Before we begin, let's remind ourselves that analysis is "the careful and close examination of the parts or elements from which something is made and how those parts affect or function within the whole to create meaning" (Burke, 2013, p. 16). In R.CCR.2, we analyzed how central ideas and themes are developed; in this anchor standard, we're analyzing the role of structure in a text. Let's organize our thinking around R.CCR.5 by looking at some of the different types of texts we might ask students to read.

STRUCTURE AND INTERCONNECTEDNESS IN NOVELS

One of our favorite novels year after year is Erich Maria Remarque's *All Quiet on the Western Front* (1929); I personally love the book for many reasons, but one of them is Remarque's inclusion of striking scenes that are at first awkward and then profound. (Remember, I teach high school freshmen—perhaps the quintessential audience for awkward moments.)

In one of the novel's early scenes, we find protagonist Paul sitting in a meadow with a couple of his comrades-in-arms. Everything is pleasant about the scene—they are sitting in a circle, playing cards, laughing, talking—except for two jarring details: they are sitting on boxes with holes in the tops, and their pants are around their ankles. As we closely read this passage in class, I enjoy watching my students' faces as, one after another, it dawns on them that these men are sitting in a circle together while relieving their bowels.

Once we get through with the scene, I begin to ask my students some questions:

- Knowing that Remarque wrote this novel "to tell about men destroyed by war" (p. i), why might this scene merit inclusion here?

- Is this scene vulgar? Why or why not?

I give them a chance to propose hypotheses in pairs, and then we go back into the scene, pencils in hands, and closely read it again with our questions as a focus. I remind students that to understand how this scene relates to the novel as a whole, we'll have to look not just at what the scene says but also at what it hints at and what it doesn't explicitly say. In teacher-speak, we'll need to infer (R.CCR.1).

When we closely read the scene for the second time, students notice that this isn't such a pleasant scene after all: there are references to the nearby war front, to badly wounded Kemmerich, and to Paul and his friends' experiencing moments when there's nothing they can say. After we're finished, I have students ask three questions that they're curious about; a big question I'm hoping to see connects back to R.CCR.5: What on earth could have made these once-civilized students into callous, crude, I-seem-to-care-more-about-getting-double-rations-than-I-do-about-the-deaths-of-half-my-company young men?

Through asking the right questions, my students are led to discover that this scene is not flippant, but rather hints at a theme of the book: namely, that World War I was unlike anything humanity had ever seen, and it annihilated its participants in death and life.

For longer narrative structures like novels, R.CCR.5 envisions students who are able to piece together why seemingly disparate events are placed where they are placed by the author. In this case, the scene comes early in the book, creating growing suspense as readers start to wonder how Paul and his friends incurred such psychological damage and how they could possibly lose more of their humanity than they already have.

STRUCTURE AND INTERCONNECTEDNESS IN ARTICLES

Let's take a look at a columnist who consistently produces cogent, passionate, debate-inducing arguments every week: Leonard Pitts Jr. Whether you agree with his views or not, his writing hits on a variety of current topics, and it does a lot of work with few words. Many, if not all, of the reading anchor standards could be taught using the work of columnists like Pitts.

For the purposes of this discussion, let's look at Pitts's piece "America, the Stupid Giant, Is Evolving Backward" (2011). In the column, Pitts makes an argument, but his structure is a far cry from that of the standard six-paragraph essay I teach students to write in on-demand writing situations. One way to tackle this text in light of R.CCR.5 could be by asking students to answer these questions after an initial reading:

- What is Pitts's argument?

- If you had to choose one part of this column where Pitts summarizes his argument, where would it be? In other words, what acts as a thesis statement? (Students could argue that it's the title, or that it is contained in other parts of the column.)

- Where does Pitts address people who might be prone to disagree with him? How does he respectfully address what Graff and Birkenstein (2014) have called his "naysayers" (p. 78)?

- How does Pitts give this piece a sense of beginning and closing? In other words, which parts of the column act like an intro and a conclusion, respectively?

- What does X sentence do for the piece as a whole? How does X reference contribute to Pitts's argument?

These questions all get to how different parts of a text relate to one another. As a side note, this text lends itself to a debate that students get passionate about quickly: Is America a stupid giant, as Pitts suggests?

STRUCTURE AND INTERCONNECTEDNESS IN POEMS

Even more so than columns like Pitts's, poems do an incredible amount of sophisticated work in very little space. They are, in the words of Nancie Atwell, "cut to the bone" (2002, p. 136). My primary goal in teaching through the occasional poem, then, is not to mold my students into future English majors, but rather to equip them with the ability to see the impact of various writer moves; in the case of R.CCR.5, that's the strategic use of structure.

Take, for instance, William Stafford's poem "Fifteen" (1998), which my students and I read to kick off one of our units in Freshman Composition and Literature. After reading this poem through several times, I will ask my students some questions to get them seeing how this poem holds together.

Here are some potential questions to ask students with poetry and R.CCR.5 in mind:

- What words are repeated throughout the poem? How does this repetition give us a glimpse into what this poem is getting at?

- How long is each stanza? Why do you think Stafford made the final stanza so brief?

- Does this poem contain a turn—that is, a place in which the narrative shifts direction? If so, where? How does this turn give us insight into the poem's theme?

There is plenty of space here for me to push each of my students to think analytically, and I must model for them how poets use structure in clever, powerful ways.

STRUCTURE AND INTERCONNECTEDNESS IN PRIMARY SOURCE DOCUMENTS

If you're in a history classroom, your students are certainly required to do the primary source–reading work of historians. Considering structure with primary source documents initially means answering simple questions about text type:

- Is this an argument?

- A treatise?

- A satire?

- A legal document?

- A law?

- A court ruling?

Students should be expected to attempt to answer these kinds of questions on their own, using the text's structure as evidence for their assertions. To increase the complexity of these tasks, teachers may give students two or more interconnected primary source documents, asking students to discern how and why the texts inform one another and how they help readers explore overarching historical questions. For example, a colleague of mine (Erica Beaton) gives her students various maps, photographs, reports, and textual excerpts surrounding the Dust Bowl, and asks them to marshal these interconnected texts in a response to the question, What caused the Dust Bowl?[1]

---

1. For more from Beaton, see her excellent blog at www.b10lovesbooks.wordpress.com. The document-based question that her assignment derives from is a free sample of the Document-based Question (DBQ) Project, and you can access it at www.dbqproject.com/sg_userfiles/sample_dustbowl.pdf.

STRUCTURE AND INTERCONNECTEDNESS IN TEXTBOOKS

This one may seem obvious to some, but many students in content-area classes are next to clueless about how textbooks are designed to support learning new content. Once teachers explain the function of the structure of a textbook and the connections between its elements, students will have a much easier time understanding the information it conveys.

The explicit structure of most textbooks allows them to be read in waves.

When reading a chapter, students can be directed, first, to read text features, such as the headings, subheadings, infographics, illustrations, and review questions, which will give them a preview of the material and help them build an initial mental outline. They then read the text itself, using its details to flesh out the mental outline they created using the previewed features. Finally, they can review the text features previewed initially, this time for the purpose of determining how the author has used the structure of the textbook chapter to show the relationships between key concepts and terms.

WHY IS THIS IMPORTANT?

At its core, this standard helps students internalize the idea that there are many ways to organize one's communication. Within narrative structures, scenes can be chosen and ordered in a manner that achieves intangible effects like suspense or mystery. In argumentative pieces, central claims can be delivered anywhere within the piece, and the placement of these claims and their supporting data (pieces of evidence) and warrants (explanations of why the data supports the claim) affect the persuasiveness of the writer's position. And when explaining a concept or an idea, an author has many structures at her disposal with which to most clearly and effectively do so.

As with so many of the Common Core anchor standards, excellence in R.CCR.5 bleeds over into excellence not only in the other reading standards but in the writing, speaking and listening, and language standards as well. Those able to analyze an author's use of structure are able to think critically about their own use of structure in communicating, whether through speaking or through writing.

The 6th college and career readiness anchor standard within the reading strand of the CCSS reads as follows:

> Assess how point of view or purpose shapes the content and style of a text.

In other words, how does where a writer or narrator is coming from (point of view) or going toward (purpose) affect what she writes (content and style)?

POINT OF VIEW

Whether reading literature or informational texts, college- and career-ready people consider the vantage point of the speaker. In a story, this is a question of the narrator's point of view, which is often categorized by how much the narrator knows (first person, third person limited, third person omniscient) and the narrator's trustworthiness.

There is also a cultural element to point of view, and some of the grade-level iterations of R.CCR.6 try to emphasize this by explicitly calling for diverse reading. For example, R.9–10.6 (the version of this anchor standard specifically written for ninth and tenth graders) says, "Analyze a particular point of view or cultural experience reflected in a work of literature from outside the United States, drawing on a wide reading of world literature." A fine example of this is in our earlier discussion of R.CCR.4—students could examine Kipling's poem and Achebe's novel as two points of view on colonialism, only this time taking it a step further and considering how each writer's cultural background affects his perspective.

Point of view is interesting, also, in history classes, especially when reading seemingly neutral explanatory texts. Students can read two accounts of the same time period or event, paying attention to which details are excluded and which are emphasized in each telling. Such examinations often shock students as they truly realize, for the first time, that any given textbook chapter represents hundreds of choices: what to keep, what to exclude, what to put in bold print as a key concept, and so on.

PURPOSE

It is almost impossible to separate a writer's point of view from his purpose. Purposes can be roughly categorized, as they have been for years, into four main aims: to inform, to persuade, to express, or to entertain. But college- and career-ready people detect greater nuance than these four categories allow. Writing to inform differs from writing to explain, and writing to persuade is different from writing to inspire. These four main distinctions are useful, however, and lacking an awareness of them can lead to a reader's disagreeing with a piece that was simply written for expression, or arguing with a text meant solely for entertainment.

HOW DO POINT OF VIEW AND PURPOSE SHAPE LITERARY TEXTS?

Point of view and purpose have a powerful shaping effect on texts. For example, in J. D. Salinger's *The Catcher in the Rye* (1951), Holden Caulfield frequently speaks in the passive voice, and we can infer that his fear of adulthood may contribute to this. He also uses the phrase "sort of" over one hundred times in the novel. This distance-creating, noncommittal language use grows from Holden's point of view as someone very afraid of growing up (Green, 2013).

Point of view and purpose are worth time in the classroom only if the time goes beyond teaching point of view as just another literary term. Asking students to identify whether John Knowles's *A Separate Peace* (1959) is written in the first person or the third person is mundane and nearly useless; questions like this don't answer a "So what?" and often seem disconnected from any type of applicable knowledge or skill.

What if point of view questions looked more like these?

- In Knowles's *A Separate Peace*, an adult Gene tells of his years at

Devon. Yet, considering Gene's deep involvement in the story's key conflict, is Gene a reliable narrator? Give evidence to support your answer.

- In Remarque's *All Quiet on the Western Front* (1929), there is a sudden shift between the narrator's point of view in Chapter 12 and the point of view in the two-paragraph epilogue that ends the book. What does this shift mean? Is this shift an effective way to end the novel, in your opinion?

- In Salinger's *The Catcher in the Rye*, what problems does Holden's narration present to the reader? What does it reveal about Holden's fears?

- In Achebe's *Things Fall Apart* (1959), what cultural viewpoints might Achebe be responding to? Where do you see this in Achebe's text?

Questions like these provide a critical angle from which to approach point of view, and students in grades 6 through 12 are ready to engage in this type of thinking with the proper scaffolding. Kids want to do more than identify whether a story is told in the first or the third person; they want to analyze, discuss, and debate the complex issues that point of view brings up. This anchor invites us to let them do just that.

HOW DO POINT OF VIEW AND PURPOSE SHAPE AN INFORMATIONAL TEXT?

It is worth taking an extra moment to discuss the unique ways in which point of view and purpose shape informational texts. Whether reading informational texts in the ELA classroom, analyzing documents in history class, or reading articles and reports in science class, understanding the interconnectedness of point of view and purpose is an integral part of R.CCR.6 and of preparing for life as an intelligent adult.

For example, let's consider a series of primary source documents from *The Human Record: Sources of Global History since 1500* by Andrea Overfield (2011):

- Document 1: "Agreement between Charles D. Rudd, et al., and Lobengula, King of Matabeleland, 1891" (pp. 308–309)

- Document 2: "Letter of King Lobengula to Queen Victoria" (p. 309)

- Document 3: "George Washington Williams, Open Letter to King Leopold II of Belgium, 1890" (pp. 310–312)

- Document 4: "King Leopold II, Open Letter to the Officials of the Congo Free State, 1897" (pp. 313–314)

- Document 5: "Ndansi Kumalo, His Story, Reflections of an African Warrior" (pp. 315–317)

Simple questions will get students ready to consider point of view, purpose, and these five documents separately and as a unified whole:

- Who wrote this? How do you know?

- What was the purpose of this document? How do you know?

    For example, in document 2, the purpose is to seek justice for the deception of document 1. Lobengula is informing Rudd's queen of the deceptive conditions under which he signed Rudd's "agreement."

- How do point of view and purpose shape the style of each of these documents?

For example, in document 3, Williams is writing to his friend, who also happens to be a powerful king, but he is extremely disillusioned by the difference between King Leopold's claims about the Belgian Congo and what actually is happening there; thus, his style is fascinating: he is both humble and bold, repeatedly calling King Leopold "your majesty" but also being brutally honest about the despicable conditions in the Congo.

These types of questions are great fodder for both discussion and writing. They beg the habitual use of textual evidence, a thread woven through many of the anchor standards. As is often the case, once you get an overall grasp of the standards, you will find that you're hitting a lot of the specific standards without even knowing it.

WHY IS THIS IMPORTANT?

At the heart of this anchor standard is reading between the lines and determining what forces are truly shaping a text. Although postsecondary life may not present non–English majors with many assigned novels, it will present them with plenty of "texts" profoundly shaped by their source and their purpose: articles, advertisements, infomercials, websites, conversations. College- and career-ready people are prepared to instinctively "read" everything from the angle of point of view and purpose so that they can make informed decisions on everything from which company to work for to which politician to vote for.

The 7th college and career readiness anchor standard within the reading strand of the CCSS reads as follows:

> Integrate and evaluate content presented in diverse media and formats, including visually and quantitatively, as well as in words.

This is essentially the research standard within the reading anchor standards, and it is closely linked to the "Research to Build and Present Knowledge" writing anchor standards (W.CCR.7–9) and the "Comprehension and Collaboration" speaking and listening anchor standards (SL.CCR.1–3). All of these standards point to the skills necessary for gathering, assessing, and applying information from diverse media formats, including print and digital sources like video and audio clips.

EVALUATE CONTENT

Many have said that one of the most important skills of the twenty-first century is determining whether the website you're looking at is reliable or not. When we do this, I tell students, we are evaluating a site's reliability. When we evaluate something, we determine if it is good or bad, or right or wrong (Marzano & Simms, 2013, p. 66).

As an example of evaluating Web content, when I Google "Common Core," there are various tiers of trustworthiness and usability that I use to subconsciously filter the search results; you probably do something similar:

- Tier 1 information is directly from www.corestandards.org, the official home page of the CCSS. This information comes directly from the authors of the standards, and therefore has that "straight from the source" authority. It is also limited, however, in that it's only presented with one voice; there's nothing personal about www.corestandards .org, and by its very nature it offers little guidance for people looking for Common Core implementation solutions.

- Tier 2 information, in my mind, includes information about the CCSS posted in journals; foundation-sponsored publications; and other authoritative, professionally edited sources. *Education Week* is a good example of such a source. Information sources in this tier are unlikely to be error ridden; but they can contain bias, and, due to the professional level of the publication, this bias may be tricky to spot.

- Tier 3 information includes information about the CCSS posted on blogs (like *Teaching the Core*), in tweets, on Facebook, on wikis, and so on. There's a lot of great information contained within these sources, but due to their lack of editorial oversight, they also tend to contain misinformation or bias. In addition, there's an enormous amount of this material, so it can be a bit difficult to navigate.

I'll sometimes discuss these tiers of reliability with my students to aid them in research tasks. When doing this, here are some questions we may explore:

- How do I detect bias in a text?
- How do I determine who published a document?
- Which tier or tiers of information are valid for gaining background knowledge on a topic?
- Which tier or tiers are valid for supporting a formal argument?

And here it's worth noting that, though the CCSS envision students who know how to evaluate content, they don't dictate how teachers should teach students to arrive at this skill. This leaves room for professional judgment, which I like; if you're unsure of where to begin, however, I recommend Christopher Lehman's approach (2012, p. 24): he models for students how he "look(s) backward (and when needed...forward) to see if the author's ideas are clearly supported...or if they feel weak or missing."

EVALUATE *DIVERSE* CONTENT

Another aspect of R.CCR.7 is the need for students to grapple with diverse content. I just outlined my process for evaluating online information, but the grade- and subject-specific versions of R.CCR.7 help us get a better picture of the types of diverse content a college-

and career-ready person should be able to grapple with:

- "Analyze the representation of a subject or a key scene in two different artistic mediums, including what is emphasized or absent in each treatment (e.g., Auden's 'Musee des Beaux Arts' and Brueghel's 'Landscape with the Fall of Icarus')" (RL.9–10.7).

- "Analyze various accounts of a subject told in different mediums (e.g., a person's life story in both print and multimedia), determining which details are emphasized in each account" (RI.9–10.7).

- "Integrate quantitative or technical analysis (e.g., charts, research data) with qualitative analysis in print or digital text" (RH.9–10.7).

- "Translate quantitative or technical information expressed in words in a text into visual form (e.g., a table or chart) and translate information expressed visually or mathematically (e.g., in an equation) into words" (RST.9–10.7).

These examples, which treat this standard in literature, informational texts, history and social studies, and science and technical subjects, respectively, help illustrate the range of content college- and career-ready people should be able to evaluate. Whether we are viewing a painting, a film, a YouTube video, a statistical graph, an equation, or a political cartoon, the goal is to develop a habitually analytical eye for any informational nugget we come across.

INTEGRATE IT ALL

Finally, the last crucial skill within R.CCR.7 is bringing all of this information together. We integrate things when we "combine different perspectives from various media into a coherent understanding or position about the subject" (Burke, 2013, p. 46). In other words:

- How do we take selections from the various abovementioned tiers of online Common Core information and turn them into a coherent understanding of the standards?

- How do we read a textbook chapter about divine right monarchs, view their official portraits, read Rousseau's scathing indictment of them, and then turn all of these readings into a coherent understanding of the divine right monarchs?

- How do we translate procedural diagrams into words, or translate written-out procedures into procedural diagrams?

WHY IS THIS IMPORTANT?

An understanding of any topic, whether it be the Common Core or parenting, is bound to be richer and more nuanced when it comes from integrating information from a variety of sources, and these sources shouldn't be limited to any one tier of reliability or type of medium. Such integration is a powerful mental habit, and those who possess it tend not merely to understand big ideas better but also to come up with ideas that are entirely new.

The 8th college and career readiness anchor standard within the reading strand of the CCSS reads as follows:

> Delineate and evaluate the argument and specific claims in a text, including the validity of the reasoning as well as the relevance and sufficiency of the evidence.

This is a fun one: picking apart arguments. Yes, fun.[1]

DELINEATING AN ARGUMENT: FOUR KEY PARTS

There are several models out there for breaking down arguments into their core parts.[2] For the sake of our discussion on this anchor, let me just share the broad pieces of an argument I work on with my high school freshmen. College- and career-ready people, as defined in the Common Core, are able to describe the following basic parts in a given argument they read, although they may not use these exact terms:

- **The claim.** This is the debatable point of the piece, boiled down to a sentence or so. Thesis statements are claims. Note that we're focusing here not on every single debatable point made in an argument, but on the primary point.

- **The evidence.** This is what backs up your argument; it essentially answers the question, What are you basing that claim on? According to R.CCR.8, a college- and career-ready person

---

1. Here are five ways I strive to make rigorous arguments enjoyable: www.teachingthecore.com/5-ways-to-make-rigorous-arguments-fun/.
2. I particularly love the clarity with which Michael Smith, Jeffrey Wilhelm, and James Fredricksen lay out Stephen Toulmin's model on page 17 of their book *Oh, Yeah?! Putting Argument to Work Both in School and Out* (2012).

needs to be able to determine how relevant and sufficient this evidence is in relation to the claim.

- **The warrant.** This is the reasoning (see the language in R.CCR.8) that connects the evidence to the claim. For example, if you are trying to argue that obesity in the United States is a national crisis, you might cite evidence indicating how much heart disease costs the American taxpayer as part of the economic prong of your argument. To effectively use this evidence, however, you would need some warrants to connect it to your claim; toward that end, you might show that heart disease has a strong correlation to obesity and also that the cost to taxpayers is sufficient to merit labeling obesity a crisis.

- **The rebuttal.** A good argument "names its naysayers" by addressing opponents and counterclaims. Effective rebuttals are respectful and accurate; they depict the other side in a fashion that the other side would agree with, and then they either disagree entirely or they make limited concessions. Note that rebuttals aren't mentioned in R.CCR.8, but most arguments contain them, and college- and career-ready people therefore are able to notice them.

To help my students grasp the basic parts of an argument, I explicitly teach and model the parts, and I involve them in in-class debates, pausing to interject when someone has created an especially strong claim or rebuttal or warrant. Debate has proven a powerful method for getting my students ready to delineate and evaluate (and create, as we'll discuss in W.CCR.1) written arguments.

To guide them in delineating an argument, I might ask these questions:

- What claim is the author making?
- What evidence does the author use to support her claim?
- What warrant(s) does the author give for using this evidence?
- How does the author handle opposing views?

EVALUATING AN ARGUMENT

Remember that evaluation involves deciding whether something is right or wrong, solid or faulty, good or bad. To guide my students in evaluating an argument, here are some additional questions I ask:

- Is the author's claim clear?
- Does the author's tone lend itself to credibility? Fanaticism? Boredom?

- Is the evidence used sufficient to support the claim? Is there enough evidence? Is it well founded? Is it from a reputable source?

  Here, it's helpful to discuss with students the limitations of evidence from personal experience. When my students first start debating or reading arguments, it's common for them to be swayed on massive issues through the speaker's or author's use of a single poignant story.

- Are the author's warrants valid? Is there enough reasoning to clearly show that the evidence supports the claim?

WHY IS THIS IMPORTANT?

If this seems like dry or overly heady stuff to you, I strongly recommend reading Graff's work—particularly *Clueless in Academe* (2003), and, as a support to that text, *They Say, I Say* (Graff & Birkenstein, 2014). The central premise of Graff's work is that argument is the unifying thread through all of academic and public discourse, and that therefore argument is the pedagogical key to unlocking the latent intellectual in each student, democratizing academia, and about fifty million other things we're banging our head against in U.S. education. In other words, if you are passionate about narrowing the achievement gap, making college accessible to all students, or simply improving the quality and usefulness of public discourse, go big on argument.

9

The 9th college and career readiness anchor standard within the reading strand of the CCSS reads as follows:

> Analyze how two or more texts address similar themes or topics in order to build knowledge or to compare the approaches the authors take.

This anchor envisions someone who is able to begin to do a basic form of what Mortimer Adler and Charles Van Doren (1972)—authors of the epically titled *How to Read a Book: The Classic Guide to Intelligent Reading*—have called "syntopical reading" (p. 309), which is reading multiple texts to gain a greater understanding of the body of knowledge to which they collectively contribute. But the anchor also envisions someone who can read works by two or more authors and compare how they approached their authorial task.

READ RELATED TEXTS

Before students can analyze related texts, they first must read them. R.CCR.9 describes texts related either topically or thematically. Let's examine a few examples of how this might look.

Topically Linked Texts from Multiple Genres

For example, as I mentioned previously, when we read Achebe's *Things Fall Apart* (1959) my ninth-grade students and I also examine Kipling's poem "The White Man's Burden" (1899); we also read open letters to and from King Leopold (Overfield, 2011) during Belgium's imperial heyday. Altogether, these texts come from various genres, and some of them contain starkly contrasting themes, but they all topically deal with colonization and imperialism around the turn of the twentieth century.

Topically Linked Articles

For finding multiple related articles about the news and issues of today, I haven't found a better resource than the *Week*—a free online news magazine (http://theweek.com). I've heard it described as the *Reader's Digest* version of the *Wall Street Journal*, and I can see why: every day, the *Week* posts articles that summarize the various takes on a given hot topic (for example, "Five Perspectives on the Disappointing Jobs Report for the USA"). There are links to the opinions being summarized, allowing teachers or students to go directly to the sources of the various opinions to read them in their entirety.

Thematically Linked Texts from Multiple Genres

But let's say you're interested in having students explore thematic relationships between texts, maybe hitting some R.CCR.7 along the way. I do something like this in our unit surrounding Knowles's *A Separate Peace* (1959). Our guiding question while reading the book is, Is Gene evil, or did he simply do an evil thing? This got us thinking and talking about the theme I wanted students to explore: Are humans basically evil, or are we all basically good people who do evil things?

Here are ideas I've used for thematically linked studies to supplement *A Separate Peace:*

- Exploring the writings on human nature of various Enlightenment thinkers

- Reading an article or excerpts from Freud dealing with the id, ego, and superego

- Studying a current events case that relates to our thematic driving question, such as the George Zimmerman and Trayvon Martin tragedy

READ RELATED TEXTS TO BUILD KNOWLEDGE

Habitual knowledge building is one of the elements that the Common Core lists as integral to college and career readiness; but because the standards seek to remain as content agnostic as possible, this fact often gets forgotten. I have heard Common Core naysayers claim in passing that the Common Core gets rid of content knowledge, instead focusing solely on skill development. Yet in the introductory matter of the standards, the authors state:

Students establish a base of knowledge across a wide range of subject matter by engaging with works of quality and substance. They read purposefully and listen attentively to gain both general knowledge and discipline-specific expertise. They refine and share their knowledge through writing and speaking. (NGA & CCSSO, 2010, p. 7)

In other words, the standards envision schools with knowledge-rich curricula that produce knowledge-rich—not simply skillful—graduates.

I love that the CCSS make the vital connection between reading multiple sources and building knowledge. In the *Things Fall Apart* example, this is the only way my students can truly understand the complexities and the dark underbelly of colonialism; they need to get elbow deep in the grime of multiple, often conflicting texts.

READ RELATED TEXTS TO COMPARE AUTHORIAL APPROACHES

It's also valuable to compare how different authors approach a given topic. The task of finding informational or argumentative texts on a related theme is wonderfully aided, once again, by the *Week*. Because journalists take such a wide array of tacks toward the same topic, and because they tend to do so with such brevity, articles are a great means of comparing authorial approaches.

WHY IS THIS IMPORTANT?

Skill and knowledge are not easily separated. The more students read related texts, the more expertise and confidence they build both in the knowledge area being explored and in regard to their ability to gain knowledge in other areas. And this is more than just a feel-good skill set, as even entry-level jobs in the United States are frequently in "knowledge-intensive, dynamically changing workplace[s]" (Conley, 2014, p. 22). In short, knowledge is inextricably linked to literacy, and literacy is increasingly tied to a livable wage for Americans.

The 10th (and final!) college and career readiness anchor standard within the reading strand of the CCSS reads as follows:

> Read and comprehend complex literary and informational texts independently and proficiently.

In short, students need to be able to—on their own—understand complex texts. That, in and of itself, doesn't seem like such a big deal. But what makes this standard controversial and challenging is that each grade-level standard calls for grade-appropriate complex texts—and that grade-appropriate bar is quite high.

READ AND COMPREHEND *GRADE-APPROPRIATE* COMPLEX TEXTS

Though the anchor standard itself doesn't mention grade appropriateness, every grade-level standard within R.CCR.10 does (this book emphasizes studying the anchor standards to gain a grasp of the Common Core's aims, but there are grade-specific standards within each anchor; these serve as measurements along the way to college and career readiness). Basically, R.CCR.10 aims at students' being able to read at least at a level commensurate with their grade in school.

It's imperative not to confuse this with students' reading texts at their personal reading ability level. I think the Common Core leaves plenty of room for choice reading and reading workshop models—in fact, those models are a key method schools may use to ensure that kids grow as readers—but they also insist that we can't stop with kids' only reading texts of their choice or texts that *immediately align* with their "just right" reading zone. The reason for this is explained at length in the Common Core's Appendix A, but I'll summarize it here: though the reading demands of college and career texts have increased or remained constant over the last few decades, the reading demands placed on K–12 students during the same time period have lowered. The Common Core's solution to this problem is ensuring that K–12 reading demands gradually "staircase" up into the demands of the college and career world.

This is far from a revolutionary goal—that kids should be proficient readers on pace to read at a college- and career-ready level on leaving high school—but, thanks perhaps to the Common Core's somewhat more stringent definition of text complexity, the goal is getting quite a bit of attention, because students of every ability level are being expected to *actually read* some texts each year that are grade appropriate.

In other words, even if seventh grader Susan reads at a third-grade level, she has frequent opportunities throughout the school year and across the content areas to be taught how to read texts that are appropriately complex for the seventh grade.

I love it. Here's why.

This doesn't mean she's only allowed to read seventh-grade texts or that she's expected to read seventh-grade texts during her entire seventh-grade year *without support*; it just means that, no matter what remedial programs Susan ends up in, no matter what "track" she ends up on, no matter what labels she acquires during her journey through public education, Susan is going to get instruction on reading texts that stretch even her peers who read at grade level. Though this may at times be frustrating for Susan, it will be infinitely less frustrating than jumping out of a high school wading pool filled with puppies and goldfish into the shark tank of the career and college world. If the "staircase of complexity" is implemented as a part of Susan's K–12 education, Susan will enter the waters of postsecondary life with, at the very least, an idea of the types of texts she may be required to read (and years of instruction on how to grapple with them); to go back to the metaphor, she'll have more than swimmies when she enters the shark tank—she'll at least have years of shark-fighting training.

End "life = shark tank" metaphor.

This reasoning may seem extreme or even unkind, but I would submit that students like Susan are often killed with kindness and differentiated right to the bottom end of the achievement gap. I am all for differentiation, but not to the point where it means Susan doesn't get to read the same core texts and build the same core knowledge as her peers. Susan deserves support with grade-appropriate complex texts—not a temporary free pass from learning to read them.

The other reason I appreciate the centrality of grade-appropriate complex texts in the Common Core is that it emphasizes the power of the teacher. In the standards, we're essentially being told, "Preparing kids for the complex texts the information age will throw at them is a high priority. Let's clear away a lot of nonsense standards so that you teachers have the time and space to devote to this task." Keep in mind, please, that the task is hard—that's why we, as teachers, parents, and stakeholders, need to demand that we be allowed to focus on giving students a top-quality education. Empowering people with the high opportunity and high cost of standards like R.CCR.10 is one of the main reasons I can write with passion about the Common Core; standards like these represent an enormous opportunity, but also an enormous potential for loss if we don't implement them with focus and commitment.

Thankfully, the CCSS don't dictate how we're to accomplish the staircase of complexity. This leaves a lot of flexibility within which we, as teachers, can practice the entrepreneurship and collaboration that should be central to our profession.

A NOTE ON HOW COMMON CORE GRADE APPROPRIATENESS IS TO BE DETERMINED

There are two main ways to get a feel for what texts the CCSS would define as grade appropriate.

First, there is the list of text exemplars in the Common Core's Appendix B. In this appendix, lists of text exemplars (both informational and literary) are broken up according to grade level; and, for grades 6 through 12, informational texts are broken up into ELA; history and social studies; and math, science, and technical subjects.

Remember, this is a list of text *exemplars;* the Common Core does not dictate which texts must be read at which grade level (except in rare cases, such as the reading of documents foundational to the United States). Buyer beware: publishers seeking to capitalize on Appendix B or perhaps confused by the fact that these are only exemplars are packaging the text exemplars into grade-level sets and making them seem like *the* Common Core books for each grade level.

Second, there is a three-part "formula" that the CCSS use to determine whether a text is appropriately complex for a group of students (see Figure R.CCR.10.1). As you can see, text complexity cannot be solely determined by a computer, nor can it be solely determined by people outside of your classroom, nor can it be solely determined by you. Instead, the CCSS advocate for an equal emphasis on qualitative, quantitative, and reader and task considerations.

Qualitative
Levels of Meaning, Structure,
Language Conventionality,
Clarity, and Knowledge Demands
—Determined by humans

Quantitative
Word Length and Frequency,
Sentence Length,
and Text Cohesion
—Determined by an algorithm

Reader and Task
Student Motivation, Knowledge,
and Experiences: The Purpose and
Complexity of the Task Assigned
—Determined by the teacher

Figure R.CCR.10.1 How to Determine Common Core Text Complexity
Source: Adapted from National Governors Association Center for Best Practices & Council of Chief State School Officers. (2010). *Common Core State Standards for English language arts and literacy in history/ social studies, science, and technical subjects.* Washington, DC: Author.

Qualitative considerations include a text's levels of meaning; its structure; the degree to which its language conventions match today's; its clarity; and its knowledge demands (in other words, Does it require us to bring large amounts of background knowledge to the task of reading it?). Because making these kinds of determinations for longer texts is a daunting task, this work is ideal for teaching departments. Quantitative considerations are those that can be measured algorithmically: word length, word frequency, sentence length, and text cohesion (a common quantitative text complexity measure is the Lexile system). Reader and task considerations are the most subjective of the three; they include student motivation, how the text's knowledge demands fit with students' background knowledge and experiences, the purpose students have for reading the text, and the complexity of the task assigned with the text. These considerations are most naturally made by a child's teacher.

To me, this balanced approach makes sense. We teachers are key professionals in the evaluation of text appropriateness for our particular students, yet we need the objective, outside input offered through both algorithmic analyses of texts (quantitative measures) and collaborative, qualitative analyses of texts.

PROFICIENTLY READ BOTH INFORMATIONAL AND LITERARY TEXTS

Another key aspect of R.CCR.10 is an equal emphasis on informational and literary texts (see Table R.CCR.10.1). According to the table cited in the Common Core introductory matter but originally from the *Reading Framework for the 2009 National Assessment of Educational Progress* (NAEP), a student's reading tasks across an entire day of school should be equally split between

TABLE R.CCR.10.1 DISTRIBUTION OF LITERARY AND INFORMATIONAL PASSAGES BY GRADE IN THE 2009 NAEP READING FRAMEWORK

Grade	Literary	Informational
4	50%	50%
8	45%	55%
12	30%	70%

Source: National Assessment Governing Board. (2008). *Reading framework for the 2009 National Assessment of Educational Progress.* Washington, DC: U.S. Government Printing Office, reprinted in National Governors Association Center for Best Practices & Council of Chief State School Officers. (2010). *Common Core State Standards for English language arts and literacy in history/social studies, science, and technical subjects.* Washington, DC: Author, 5.

literary and informational texts by the fourth grade, and thereafter should shift increasingly to informational texts.

Although there has been much hype around the idea that the Common Core is set to kill a love for reading in our students by drowning them in informational texts, it's critical to emphasize that these reading distribution percentages are across a student's entire day of school, meaning that much of the shift will actually fall on social studies and science teachers.

WHY IS THIS IMPORTANT?

There is a due date on our task of equipping our students to independently grapple with the demands of college and career reading, and that due date is graduation. Too often, our students are given the "right" to choose their own reading or are handed the "just right" book, and they are being given the impression, whether intentionally or not, that college and career readiness is just one of many choices that lead to a good life. Although it is challenging to teach below-level readers to successfully navigate on-level texts, I consider this one of the great privileges of my job as an English and history teacher. It is a privilege because where much is at stake, great are the rewards, both for me and for my students.

PART III

The Anchor Standards in Writing

LET'S DOMINATE THE MIGHTY COMMON CORE WRITING ANCHOR STANDARDS, SHALL WE?
You've made it through the reading strand of anchor standards, so now it's time to tackle the anchor standards in writing. The question these anchor standards seek to answer is, What should a college- and career-ready person be able to do as a writer?

HOW ARE THE ANCHOR STANDARDS IN WRITING ORGANIZED?

The 10 anchor standards in writing are broken up into 4 groups:
1. Text Types and Purposes (W.CCR.1–3)
2. Production and Distribution of Writing (W.CCR.4–6)
3. Research to Build and Present Knowledge (W.CCR.7–9)
4. Range of Writing (W.CCR.10)

Or, in everyday human terms, these anchor standards are dedicated to answering these questions:
1. How do you write a beautiful argument? How do you explain a complex idea clearly? How do you retell a real or imagined experience well?
2. How do task, purpose, and audience alter how you write? What processes do you go through to create effective pieces of writing? In what ways does technology help (and inhibit) the production and distribution of your writing?
3. How do you conduct research for both short and extended projects? Which sources are credible? How do you integrate information from research while avoiding plagiarism?
4. Can you write in both timed and extended situations? Is your writing adaptable to a range of tasks, purposes, and audiences?

Before we move on, let me just say that, of all the areas of literacy, writing, for me and many, is the most complex and daunting to teach. By far the best professional development available for learning to effectively teach writing is that offered through the National Writing Project and its regional affiliates. I am deeply indebted to the four weeks that I spent as a fellow of the Invitational Summer Institute (ISI) of the Lake Michigan Writing Project. The ISI fellowship is offered by many of the regional writing projects around the nation, and, best of all, teachers from all grade levels and content areas may apply. I'll give one final word of warning, though: the self-directed, learn-by-doing approach of the National Writing Project and its professional development experiences will ruin you for the traditional, learn-by-sitting-and-listening professional development prevalent throughout the United States!

The 1st college and career readiness anchor standard within the writing strand of the Common Core State Standards (CCSS) reads as follows:

> Write arguments to support claims in an analysis of substantive topics or texts using valid reasoning and relevant and sufficient evidence.

Before exploring the actual standard, let's discuss the "specialness" of argument within the Common Core.

WHY IS ARGUMENTATIVE WRITING FIRST?

On page 24 of Appendix A of the CCSS there's a section called "The Special Place of Argument in the Standards" (National Governors Association Center for Best Practices [NGA] & Council of Chief State School Officers [CCSSO], 2010). It's not a long read, but it's packed with useful insights into why the authors of the CCSS gave argument (and, in the early grades, opinion writing) primacy of place in the standards. Here is my abbreviated version of the section:

- Academia is an argument culture; therefore, "argument literacy" is crucial for success in academia (Graff, 2003, p. 23).

- Argument isn't about winning; instead, it's "a serious and focused conversation among people who are intensely interested in getting to the bottom of things cooperatively" (Williams & McEnerney, n.d.).

- In the world of work, being able to back up opinions and ideas with strong evidence and sound reasoning is crucial.

- Argument has strong ties with research and knowledge building, both of which are also important within the Common Core.

- It's an important element in curriculum frameworks for numerous high-performing nations.

- It develops "capacities broadly important for the literate, educated person living in the diverse, information-rich environment of the twenty-first century" (NGA & CCSSO, 2010, p. 25).

And that's why argument comes first.

SO, WHAT'S AN ARGUMENT, ACCORDING TO THE COMMON CORE?

In that same Appendix A, we find a meaty definition of an argument:

> Arguments are used for many purposes—to change the reader's point of view, to bring about some action on the reader's part, or to ask the reader to accept the writer's explanation or evaluation of a concept, issue, or problem. An argument is a reasoned, logical way of demonstrating that the writer's position, belief, or conclusion is valid. (NGA & CCSSO, 2010, p. 23)

The explanation then explores several discipline-specific uses of argumentation:

In English language arts, students make claims about the worth or meaning of a literary work or works. They defend their interpretations or judgments with evidence from the text(s) they are writing about. In history/social studies, students analyze evidence from multiple primary and secondary sources to advance a claim that is best supported by the evidence, and they argue for a historically or empirically situated interpretation. In science, students make claims in the form of statements or conclusions that answer questions or address problems. Using data in a scientifically acceptable form, students marshal evidence and draw on their understanding of scientific concepts to argue in support of their claims. Although young children [in elementary school] are not able to produce fully developed logical arguments, they develop a variety of methods to extend and elaborate their work by providing examples, offering reasons for their assertions, and explaining cause and effect. These kinds of expository structures are steps on the road to argument. In grades K–5, the term "opinion" is used to refer to this developing form of argument.

The preceding points are useful in that they can help us show students the argument culture of academia by teaching them the ways in which arguments differ by discipline. If teachers of all of the classes and age levels become knowledgeable about the arguments in their own discipline as well as aware of the argumentative thread that weaves through academic discourse, students may begin to make sense of seemingly disconnected classes.

Now that we've got some "why" and "what" questions handled, let's look at the three core skills contained within W.CCR.1.

MAKE A CLAIM ABOUT A SUBSTANTIVE TOPIC OR TEXT

We already broke down some of the key elements of an argument back in R.CCR.8, so for the sake of explaining this standard, let's do something a little different and look at a sample assignment from one of my courses. As part of our *Odyssey* unit, my ninth-grade students read a document that compares life in Athens and life in Sparta,[1] and they argue which polis would be the better place to live.

At this point it's important to note that college- and career-ready people aren't just able to argue—they are able to argue about substantive topics or texts. In this example, my students are arguing not about a substantive text (although it's in our *Odyssey* unit, none of this argument is based on Homer's work), but, as you'll see, about substantive topics.

My purposes behind the Athens-Sparta argument are threefold:

- I want students to build knowledge about the city-states of ancient Greece. (Remember that the CCSS were not designed to "kill content"; they actually depend on a content-rich curriculum.)

- I want them to practice argumentation.

- I want them to consider substantive topics like the role of the military in society and gender equality.

Also, for the sake of making argumentation even clearer to my students,

---

1. Here is a link to the graphic organizer I share with students for the Athens and Sparta activity: https://docs.google.com/document/d/1hLXbQ_Yli6yB3pXOyoy-9aFXpx_wkPEZvj-pvJxFSns/edit.

they don't just write their arguments; they use them in a back-and-forth, whole-class, graded debate.

Once they've had time to closely read and annotate the document comparing life in Athens and life in Sparta, I ask them to decide which polis they'll be arguing for. For my indecisive students, I remind them that the best debaters are those who can argue any side of an argument, and that they do need to choose a side.

Any time my students are going to make an argument, I want them thinking about these kinds of questions when they're preparing their claim:

- Is my claim debatable? Is it intriguing? Is it clear?

  In the Athens-Sparta example, I prompt them to think about how they can enhance their claim. Instead of allowing them simply to write "Sparta would be a better place to live than Athens," I push them to consider how to strengthen their language and clarify their claim. For example, "Because I'm a woman, I would rather be dead in Sparta than alive in Athens."

- How can I ensure that my claim stays separate, in the minds of my audience, from other, similar claims?

- Do I have evidence in mind that can support my claim?

The last bullet point is key for moving on to the next skill.

SUPPORT THAT CLAIM WITH RELEVANT AND SUFFICIENT EVIDENCE

I teach my students that great arguers start with a ton of evidence, rank it in order of relevance and strength—either on paper or in their head—and then draw a line in the list where the evidence starts getting weak.

For the Athens-Sparta example, here's a brief list of prioritized evidence:

- Women in Athens were viewed as property. To live life out of the house, you had to be a priestess or a prostitute.

- Women in Sparta were educated. They could play sports.

- Although women were assigned a husband in Sparta, they were never viewed as property.

- In times of war, a Spartan woman was responsible for overseeing her husband's estate. This is a much more noble calling than being one more possession for an Athenian man.

If this were an argument based on multiple texts or a longer text, the list of evidence would be longer, and some evidence would need to be eliminated from the argument for the sake of keeping it focused.

TIE IT ALL TOGETHER WITH VALID REASONING

The reasoning (or, as we discussed in R.CCR.8, warrant) of an argument tends to answer "why" or "how" questions. I teach my student writers to anticipate such questions with prompts like these:

- Why does this piece of evidence support your claim?

- Why is your claim superior to your opponent's?

- How is your claim limited?

The last question is key for students, because they often think that argument is about winning, and that the only way to win is by making one's claim appear perfect. But, unlike some kinds of persuasive writing, argumentation is based on logic and reasoning. An argument that strategically avoids mentioning any evidence contrary to its claim is always going to be a failed argument, because the intelligent reader will smell a rat.

Now prepared with intentionally crafted arguments that advance a claim with evidence and reasoning, students read their argument drafts in pairs or triads, and then we have our whole-class, back-and-forth debate. In tying together their reading about Athens and Sparta to form written arguments that they then use in spoken debate, students are one experience closer to developing the "argument literacy" this standard aims at.

WHY IS THIS IMPORTANT?

It's hard to understate the power of a classroom in which argumentation has pride of place. Every year when I speak with former students of mine, many of them remark about how much they enjoyed our in-class debates. Similarly, when I work with early-career or pre-service teachers, I ask them if they've had any good experiences in their K–12 schooling with debate. Most shake their head, but there are always a few who rave about the government or current events course in which the teacher made argumentation a central component.

Arguments are worth embracing in all of our classrooms, not simply because the Common Core says to but also for the following reasons:

1. THEY'RE COLLABORATIVE

Arguments beg for collaboration. Whether in pairs, in triads, in teams, or as a whole class, when students are engaged with a substantive text or topic, even the most reticent kids tend to get involved.

2. THEY BUILD COMMUNITY

This might seem counterintuitive if you're thinking about arguments as solely adversarial. But arguments are more than competitive when we do them right; in fact, they're downright cooperative. Arguments are about "getting to the bottom of things," to borrow from Joseph Williams and Lawrence McEnerney (n.d.). They are an expression of our desire to get to the truth in the classroom.

3. THEY PROMOTE UPPER-LEVEL THINKING

Arguments come in high on Bloom's pyramid (1956). They require us to analyze texts, topics, and situations; they require us to evaluate the validity of claims, reasoning, and evidence; and they invite us to be creative. One watershed moment in our classroom argument culture each year is when students begin spontaneously applauding when someone stands up and makes a creative, solid, or poised argument. In one of my classes, students actually developed a special variation on applause: every time an arguer nails it, they stand up, motion with their hands as if their heads are exploding, and then fall back in their seats. Although some may find that a bit graphic, I think it's awesome—they're essentially telling the arguer, "Hey, you did such a good job that it exploded my brain."

4. THEY BUILD RESPECT, CIVILITY, AND HUMILITY

For my students to flourish in the college and career world, I know they'll need more than academic skills; they'll need character. The great thing about making arguments is that it can build some really valuable character strengths. Every year, I enjoy watching students discover that respectful arguers are more powerful than disrespectful arguers, and that arguers who are willing to concede a point are more convincing than those who stubbornly (and often stupidly) ignore any validity in an opposing claim.

Our society can always use another person who thinks of others before herself. Arguments can build that kind of humble individual.

5. THEY ARE A KEY UNIFYING PRINCIPLE ACROSS ACADEMIA

I've already mentioned this point in this book, but it's such a key idea that it merits restatement. Gerald Graff (2003) claimed that students are "clueless in academe" because the unifying principle of academia—namely, that the core disciplines are different variations of an overarching argument culture—is obscured from them. Teaching students about this culture and helping them see it is a way to make school more cohesive and sensible to them.

6. THEY ARE A LINCHPIN OF DEMOCRACY

We are in a time when George Washington's "Farewell Address" (1796) is creepy in its insightful warning against political parties. As the United States becomes increasingly polarized along party lines, we need the cooperative, collaborative, upper-level thinking, civility, and intelligence that arguments produce.

7. THEY ARE IMPORTANT FOR CAREER GROWTH

I want my students to be able to advocate for themselves; in a competitive job market, this is going to be crucial. If my kids can't show why they are a great candidate, and if they can't analyze their job search and create a winning strategy, they'll have a hard time getting a job. And if they can't use those same skills while working, they'll have a hard time advancing.

8. EVERYONE WINS IN A GOOD CLASSROOM ARGUMENT

Oh good, you're thinking: here's the obligatory positive ending. Before you write me off as trite, allow me to illustrate why this is a legit final reason.

For most of the school year, I skirt past the occasional student who, at the end of a debate, asks, "So, Mr. Stuart, which team won?" When my thoughts on building an argument culture in the classroom were still nascent, I didn't know of a decent way to determine a winner, and, for instructional purposes, I didn't really need one—kids were engaged without me dangling the victory carrot in front of them.

But a couple of years ago, during the last week of school, I gave in to my students and had them vote on the winner of one of our final debates using an online, anonymous voting system. The results were not surprising: unlike practically all of our in-class arguments during the school year, this one ended with some hurt feelings instead of an eagerness to continue the debate in the hallways.

The moral of the story, to me, is simply that my in-class debates don't need a winner—in fact, assigning a winner undermines their beauty, because winning isn't the point. At the end of a great debate, my hope is that we have all practiced the other items listed here, and we have all cooperated in getting closer to "the bottom of things."

The 2nd college and career readiness anchor standard within the writing strand of the CCSS reads as follows:

> Write informative/explanatory texts to examine and convey complex ideas and information clearly and accurately through the effective selection, organization, and analysis of content.

Although the Common Core gives special emphasis to argumentative writing, it goes without saying that all good arguments incorporate elements of explanation and storytelling (which we'll explore in W.CCR.3). In this anchor, we look at informative/explanatory writing. The Common Core's Appendix A states on page 41 that this mode of writing and argumentative writing are the two "dominant" forms of written communication in postsecondary education, and they are also dominant in the secondary stan-

dards of well-performing countries (NGA & CCSSO, 2010). In other words, although argument still has pride of place, informative/explanatory writing is ultimately inseparable from argument—after all, how can you build an argument without explaining your reasoning in the process? (Guess what I'll also be saying about narrative in the next anchor standard?) Before we get into the core skills of this anchor, however, let's look at what exactly the Common Core is referring to when referencing "informative/explanatory texts."

HOW DOES THE COMMON CORE DEFINE INFORMATIVE/ EXPLANATORY TEXTS?

Once again, I'll be heading to page 23 of Appendix A (NGA & CCSSO, 2010) for help—best to get these definitions straight from the document's supporting materials. Informative/explanatory writing seeks to accurately "convey information." Its purposes are

- To increase knowledge of a subject
- To increase understanding of a procedure or process

If you're like me, you benefit from concrete examples when trying to wrap your mind around general descriptions like that just given. Here are some sample prompts from Appendix A; imagine asking your students to write informative/explanatory pieces in response to these (NGA & CCSSO, 2010, p. 23):

- What are the different types of poetry?
- What are the parts of a motor?
- How big is the United States?
- What is an X-ray used for?
- How do penguins find food?
- How does the legislative branch of the government function?
- Why do some authors blend genres?

Here are some examples I have tried with my freshman world history students:

- How did Alexander the Great Hellenize the Middle East?
- Why was Genghis Khan so militarily successful?

- What were the positive and negative aspects of the Pax Romana?
- What were the main causes of the genocides of the twentieth century?
- What were the main causes and effects of World War II?
- Why did Mao Zedong set the Cultural Revolution in motion?
- Why did the USSR collapse?
- What led European Christians to engage in the Crusades?

WHAT GENRES FALL UNDER THE UMBRELLA GENRE OF INFORMATIVE/ EXPLANATORY WRITING?

As you're probably surmising, informative/explanatory writing contains many specific genres within its broad contours. Here are some that Appendix A includes (NGA & CCSSO, 2010, p. 23):

ACADEMIC GENRES

- literary analyses
- scientific and historical reports
- summaries
- précis writing

WORKPLACE AND FUNCTIONAL GENRES

- instructions
- manuals
- memos
- reports
- applications
- résumés

HOW DOES INFORMATIVE/ EXPLANATORY WRITING DIFFER FROM ARGUMENTATIVE WRITING?

Both W.CCR.1 and W.CCR.2 call for writing that provides information, and as a result the line between them can become a bit blurry. In my own district's secondary social studies professional learning community, when we look at student samples of argumentative and informative/explanatory writing, we sometimes get to the point where we have to remind ourselves how the two differ, exactly (at least, I do). Appendix A provides some help in keeping the two straight.

With argumentative writing, the aim is to get people to believe that something is true. With explanations, the aim is to answer "why" or "how" questions, because truthfulness is assumed. Argument seeks to persuade; explanation seeks to create understanding. As I've already said, great arguments obviously contain elements of great explanations (warrants are essentially explanations), and great explanations contain elements of great arguments (namely, evidence).

Compare these three writing prompts:

- Was Alexander the Great truly great?
- How did Alexander the Great Hellenize the Middle East?
- Why did Alexander the Great Hellenize the Middle East?

Notice how the first prompt brings up a debatable point; to tackle it, the writer will have to analyze available evidence, come to her own conclusion, and then marshal the evidence to advance her claim. In the second prompt, the spread of Hellenism is not debatable, and evidence will need to be collected and marshaled to effectively and efficiently explain the process of Hellenization to a reader. Yet in the third, there is a bit more room for debate, mostly because there is more than one correct answer. A truly informative/explanatory response would lay out all probable motives without choosing one; a more argumentative response would claim that one motive was greater than all the rest.

Now that we've put a bit of flesh on our understanding of what informative/explanatory texts are and how they differ from argumentative texts, let's dive into the skills college- and career-ready folks bring together to produce this kind of writing.

SELECT, ORGANIZE, AND ANALYZE CONTENT

There are three main skills that W.CCR.2 mentions: selecting, organizing, and analyzing content. When selecting the content he'll include in an explanatory piece, a college- and career-ready person is picky. He knows that, when explaining the causes and effects of World War II, he's not writing about battles (even though he may be interested by them), and he's also not giving a country-by-country analysis. Therefore, he picks key content with which to develop his explanation.

Organizing one's explanation is also a college and career readiness skill. When writing an email to her boss explaining what she's accomplished this week, a college- and career-ready person

thinks carefully about how to organize her message. She might create a paragraph for each of her several roles with the company, or she might organize her explanation by day.

Finally, a college- and career-ready explanation includes an analysis of the content being explained. (When explaining analysis to students, my colleague Erica Beaton has them imagine pulling apart a cotton ball to examine its strands closely, thus gaining a greater understanding of the cotton ball as a whole.) If a student argues that the rise of Adolf Hitler is a cause of World War II, she should be able to methodically examine Hitler's rise while explaining how it led to the onset of war, essentially picking Hitler's career apart (analysis) and connecting each piece to World War II's beginnings. If the previously mentioned email writer decides to go with day-by-day organization, she might include an analysis of whether each day's work realized its potential or not.

MAINTAIN ACCURACY AND CLARITY

With careful content selection, organization, and analysis, the college- and career-ready person is able to produce a clear and accurate explanation of a given topic, whether it be academic or career related. Accuracy, on the one hand, refers to one's ability to represent a concept, process, or event without giving the wrong impression or misrepresenting facts. For example, saying that World War II was a bad time in world history is a bit inaccurate because it so understates the horrors of the conflict; at the same time, saying the war involved the deaths of tens of millions of Americans is inaccurate in that it does not correctly represent the number of deaths of American citizens.

Clarity, on the other hand, is primarily achieved through the use of explanatory tools, such us concrete details or analogies. Concrete details are specific details: rather than saying, "This product line is a waste of our company's time" or "The U.S. government spends a large amount of money," an effective informative/explanatory piece would list the product line's deficiencies in terms of real, measurable numbers, or it would list the United States' growth in debt per day or the rate of increase in government annual spending. Analogies are used to show how two things are similar. In the product line example, this might be done through likening the wasteful product line to a child heading to the street to sell lemonade in the middle of a blizzard; in the U.S. national debt example, an analogy might be made to a household in which spouses can't agree on a budget and thus go on spending money as they wish. The goal in using concrete details and analogies is always to further the informative/explanatory purpose of the piece, making one's concept as clear as possible.

WHY IS THIS IMPORTANT?

In an age when information multiplies exponentially each year, the ability to select, organize, and analyze content for the sake of clearly and accurately explaining a concept will only increase in value to both professors and employers. Though some who initially hear the term "informative/explanatory writing" may fear that such writing is lifeless and dull, those who explain things well make information powerful and accessible for others—and these are the only kinds of people able to navigate academia or a vertical career track.

W.CCR.
3

The 3rd college and career readiness anchor standard within the writing strand of the CCSS reads as follows:

> Write narratives to develop real or imagined experiences or events using effective technique, well-chosen details, and well-structured event sequences.

This is the final mode of writing within the big three (the other two being argumentative and informative/explanatory). Before we get to it, keep in mind that great arguments and explanations often contain stories—so don't go and get the message that just because argument has a special place in the standards and informative/explanatory writing is a dominant mode of writing in postsecondary settings, somehow narrative isn't important. It is.

With that said, let's get started.

HOW DOES THE COMMON CORE DEFINE NARRATIVE WRITING?

Appendix A is again helpful in getting a grasp of W.CCR.3. According to page 23 (NGA & CCSSO, 2010), narrative writing

- "Conveys real or imagined experiences"
- "Uses time as its [predominant] structure"

Narrative writing can be used for a variety of purposes, such as

- "To inform"
- "To instruct"
- "To persuade"
- "To entertain"

In English language arts (ELA), narrative writing can include texts from a variety of genres, comprising

- "Creative fictional stories"
- "Memoirs"

- "Anecdotes"
- "Autobiographies"

Here is a list of narrative skills that students should learn, particularly in the ELA classroom:

- "Provide visual details of scenes, objects, or people"
- "Depict specific actions (e.g., movements, gestures, postures, and expressions)"
- "Use dialogue and interior monologue that provide insight into the narrator's and characters' personalities and motives"
- "Manipulate pace to highlight the significance of events and create tension and suspense"

In history and social studies, students should

- "Write narrative accounts about individuals"
- "Construct event models of what happened, selecting from their sources only the most relevant information"

In science, students should

- "Write narrative descriptions of the step-by-step procedures they follow in their investigations"
- Write procedures in a manner that allows others to effectively "replicate their procedures and (perhaps) reach the same results"

Now let's break down the core skills in W.CCR.3.

DEVELOP REAL OR IMAGINED EXPERIENCES

First of all, the college- and career-ready person is able to create narratives of either real or imagined experiences of events. The ability to craft effective fiction or a memoir—to tell stories well, whether they're real or imagined—requires a gamut of intellectual processes from both sides of the brain, as we'll see in the following paragraphs. Proficiency at crafting fiction transfers well into arenas outside of the literary; great communicators invent stories all the time, and mini-narratives are often central in explaining a concept, arguing about policies, creating humor, or selling a product. Yet none of this helps us know how, exactly, these kinds of experiences are developed effectively; let's keep going.

USE WELL-CHOSEN DETAILS

We've all sat there and listened to someone tell us a story with unimportant details included. Unfortunately, overdetailing a story tends to kill it, and the college- and career-ready person is aware of this.

As a young boy who aspired to write novels, I included details in my stories like the color of the main character's T-shirt or the brand of his shoes. A college- and career-ready person knows that those details *can* serve a purpose in a narrative—for example, if the character is wearing a pair of Jimmy Choos (I had to Google "expensive shoes" for that one), then I, after doing some Googling, could learn she's managed to acquire a costly pair of kicks—but they realize that these details should be chosen for better reasons than simply being descriptive. In other words, college- and career-ready people know the difference between a telling detail and a pointless detail.

USE WELL-STRUCTURED EVENT SEQUENCES

One reason college- and career-ready folks don't include extraneous details in their writing is that they need to maintain a sequence of events that build on one another and, ultimately, create a unified whole. The goal is to create narratives that, in the words of the eleventh- and twelfth-grade-specific version of this anchor standard (W.11–12.3.C), "build toward a particular tone and outcome (e.g., a sense of mystery, suspense, growth, or resolution)."

The idea here is that events should fit together to create broad effects in a reader's mind—so, just like details, they should be well chosen.

USE EFFECTIVE TECHNIQUE

By the time he graduates high school, the college- and career-ready person should be comfortable using a variety of narrative techniques, such as dialogue, pacing, description, reflection, and multiple plotlines. Many of these techniques are likely to begin to be developed in the earliest grades, whereas others (such as multiple plotlines) may come into play much later.

HOW SHOULD THE THREE COMMON CORE MODES OF WRITING BE BALANCED?

If you're a non-ELA teacher reading this book, you're probably saying,

"Seriously? I'm responsible for teaching students how to incorporate multiple plotlines into a narrative? It's going to be challenging enough equipping my students with the argumentative and explanatory skills these standards call for—now you want me to work with them on dialogue, too?"

Thankfully, the introductory matter of the Common Core (NGA & CCSSO, 2010, p. 5) also includes a breakdown of the emphasis that each of the "big three" should be given during grades 4, 8, and 12 (see Table W.CCR.3.1). You'll notice that narrative writing is decreasingly prevalent as a student progresses through K–12 education, and argumentative writing and informative/explanatory writing are increasingly prevalent. The percentages in the table represent the distribution of writing across a student's entire year in all of his classes. It's also critical to note that in grades 6 through 12, narrative writing as its own, separate standard only exists for ELA. For the literacy standards outside of ELA, W.CCR.3 simply does not exist in isolation; instead, it's made explicit (for example, in the note on page 65 [NGA & CCSSO, 2010]) that making historical arguments, for instance, involves some use of efficient narration to retell key parts of significant events, or in science, as another example, that writing lab reports requires the ability to recount the procedures used to achieve one's results.

TABLE W.CCR.3.1 DISTRIBUTION OF COMMUNICATIVE PURPOSES BY GRADE IN THE 2011 NAEP WRITING FRAMEWORK

GRADE	TO PERSUADE	TO EXPLAIN	TO CONVEY EXPERIENCE
4	30%	35%	35%
8	35%	35%	30%
12	40%	40%	20%

Source: National Assessment Governing Board. (2007). Writing framework for the 2011 National Assessment of Educational Progress (Pre-publication ed.). Iowa City, IA: ACT, reprinted in National Governors Association Center for Best Practices & Council of Chief State School Officers. (2010). Common Core State Standards for English language arts and literacy in history/social studies, science, and technical subjects. Washington, DC: Author, 5.

WHY IS THIS IMPORTANT?

A skillfully constructed story can enliven a conversation, finish a sale, or shine light on a complex concept; those able to construct stories at the level of sophistication described in W.CCR.3 have the power to entertain, to inspire, or to instruct. At its core, W.CCR.3 is about not simply the skills involved in writing in certain story-driven genres, but more generally the skills required to communicate well with other human beings.

W.CCR.

4

The 4th college and career readiness anchor standard within the writing strand of the CCSS reads as follows:

> Produce clear and coherent writing in which the development, organization, and style are appropriate to task, purpose, and audience.

W.CCR.4 is simply about the communicative soul of writing; it's about ensuring, through a focus on three primary considerations, that your idea moves from your brain into the brain of another person. With any given piece of writing, the decisions that a writer must make are dictated by task, audience, and purpose (or, as I've heard them referred to, TAP).

TASK

Throughout their freshman year, my students will write many arguments in my class; sometimes these will be extended, multidraft pieces of writing, and sometimes they will be on-demand writing.

The purpose of providing both long and short time frames for writing is not merely to prepare them for the ACT writing test; more important, it's to get them used to seeing **time** as a central element of task. A college- and career-ready person thinks, *On the one hand, if I have several weeks to complete a multi-draft argument, it had better be top notch and polished until shining. On the other hand, if I have only thirty to sixty minutes to complete an argument* [as is the case with the ACT writing test, college blue book examinations, and many work-related instances of communication], *I had better accept that the writing will not be perfect, yet it should still be organized and clear. And finally, if I've procrastinated on that paper I had four weeks to work on and now it's due tomorrow, I need to adjust my expectations for the quality of the piece for the sake of getting it done.* As my colleague Erica Beaton often reminds me, "Done is better than perfect."

In many college and career situations, there is a large amount of writing to be done (papers, reports, emails), and the college- and career-ready person is able to "triage" these writing demands by thinking in terms of the task required. For example, she will spend less time on the email to a friend and more time on the midterm paper—but that leads us into the consideration of audience.

AUDIENCE

Audience is also a crucial consideration in any piece of writing. If I am writing an email to my boss, the style of the email will be considerably more formal than that of an email to my wife; if my students are writing a post to an online discussion forum with their classmates, I will expect different stylistic choices than I would in their thank-you letters to people who make donations to our classroom.

Similarly, when they are writing literary analyses that only their peers and I will read, I will model an academic style for them to mimic, and I will show them how to cite quotations in MLA format, whereas if they are composing a "letter to the editor"–style argument, we'll consider how a public audience differs from an academic one. These are just a few examples of the many different ways in which the intended audience can help shape the writing style.

PURPOSE

Purpose is the third part of TAP, and it, too, is going to shape a piece of writing. When I occasionally query magazine editors about freelance article ideas, my purpose is to sell an idea, and this totally influences my organization and style: I've got to be efficient in showing the value of my idea. Meanwhile, if I'm writing a proposal to my department for a new achievement measurement I think we should use, I am going to choose evidence and language that I think will prove to them, again, the value of my idea; efficiency will still be important, but the decision I'm asking them to make calls for thoroughness, too.

WHY IS THIS IMPORTANT?

Understanding TAP is hugely liberating for the college- and career-ready person; it frees her from trying to make every piece of writing serve every possible purpose—she knows this isn't possible, and so she saves time and energy by focusing on the unique demands of a given piece. This way of thinking helps her with every piece of writing she sits down to compose for the rest of her life: love letters, résumés, master's theses, time off requests, blog entries, or whatever else. As a result, she writes more pieces than the person without a grasp of TAP, and those pieces tend to be of better communicative value.

W.CCR. 5

The 5th college and career readiness anchor standard within the writing strand of the CCSS reads as follows:

> Develop and strengthen writing as needed by planning, revising, editing, rewriting, or trying a new approach.

A college- and career-ready person knows that effective writing is so much more than sitting down, putting fingers to keyboard, and pounding out a piece in one sitting. Whether writing arguments, explanations, narratives, or something else, there's a lot that goes into elevating a piece to its potential.

THE NOT-SO-SEXY PARTS OF THE WRITING PROCESS

To put it another way, W.CCR.5 is about the not-so-sexy parts of the writing process. If an awesome, published piece of writing can be likened to that ridiculously fit dude with the twelve-pack abs on the front of a men's fitness magazine, then W.CCR.5 is the hours of daily workouts, the careful eating choices, and the Photoshop tweaks that take place before that picture goes to print.

In short, the writing process is the hard work that makes effective writing effective. So what core skills are involved in W.CCR.5? Let's take a look.

PLAN

A college- and career-ready person rarely sits down and immediately launches into the first paragraph; he plans a piece of writing before fully carrying it out.

Here are some questions I might ask my students when they are planning a piece of writing within one of the "big three" Common Core modes of writing.

FOR AN ARGUMENT

- What is the central claim of your argument?

- What evidence will you use to support your argument?
- How will you explain the connection between your evidence and your claim?
- What arguments might your naysayers use?
- Is there any validity in your naysayers' claims? How might you acknowledge this validity while still refuting their claims?

FOR AN INFORMATIVE/EXPLANATORY PIECE

- What is the central idea, concept, event, or process that you're trying to explain?
- What details might you include to help illustrate your idea, concept, event, or process?
- What details might you exclude to help keep your piece focused?

FOR A NARRATIVE

- What are the key events or scenes of your narrative?
- How can you tie the scenes together?
- What event will your narrative build toward? What is its climax?
- How and when will you describe your characters? How and when will you describe your setting?

The point of questions like these is to help students internalize the kinds of things college- and career-ready people tend to do automatically as they write.

REVISE

Revision is, literally, re-seeing something; for me, it's about getting my students to make thorough, big-picture changes to their writing. Here are some questions I might use to help them with revision.

FOR AN ARGUMENT

- Is your claim clear? Is it fully supported with evidence?
- Do you accurately summarize your opponents' arguments?
- Do you convincingly refute the arguments of your opponents?

FOR AN INFORMATIVE/EXPLANATORY PIECE

- How could you restructure your piece to make it clearer for your reader?
- Are there any paragraphs that don't help explain your concept? What information could you replace them with to increase your reader's comprehension of the topic?

FOR A NARRATIVE

- Does your story drag in places?
- Does your dialogue seem natural and genuine, or is it stilted?

- Do your descriptions blend with the writing, or are they clunky?

Basically, college- and career-ready folks don't "one and done" a piece of writing if they want it to be awesome—they reread it and consider questions like those just listed.

EDIT

People vary in their definitions of editing, but the anchor standard seems to suggest something like copyediting, which is akin to going through a piece of writing with a fine-tooth comb. It is surface-level correction. I always seem to be tweaking my approach to teaching editing.

Whether we like it or not, employers and professors don't tend to count conventional, error-free writing as a small portion of determining a piece of writing's worth. Therefore, college- and career-ready people are unquestionably able to edit for surface-level errors, and, as with every other skill emphasized in the Common Core, they are able to do this independently.

REWRITE OR TRY A NEW APPROACH

My writing process, and that of every writer I know of, involves the hard work of rewriting. I tend to write a preliminary draft (I sometimes refer to these first drafts as "barf drafts"); leave it for a bit; and then come back, reread it, and make revisions. There are often three main areas where I find the need to rewrite or try a new approach:

- The intro
- The conclusion
- A clunky part (scientific, right?)

Intros and conclusions—or, as Jeff Anderson (2011, p. 113) calls them, "frames"—are tricky; they often somewhat echo each other, but this echoing is most effectively done with a light touch. Because I usually write my intro way before my conclusion, I tend to find, during the rereading process, that the two do not match each other at all. To add to that, there's also the "writing as discovery" thing: it's often in the midst of writing a piece that I discover what I'm really writing about.

Because of this, I often find that my intros and conclusions need more than a few strokes of revision; more times than not, they need to be rewritten completely—and that's the element of the writing process we're talking about.

Also, for someone to be ready to do anything she'd like with her writing, an eye or ear for "clunkiness" is useful. (Even as I write this, I'm suddenly horrified that I'm going to clunkily explain clunkiness.) A "clunky" part in our writing is a spot in which the prose becomes mired in wordiness or awkwardness or redundancy. The best way to help our students detect such areas is by modeling for them how we, first, detect clunkiness in our writing, and then, second, rewrite clunky parts in an attempt to improve the prose.

In short, a college- and career-ready person is able to identify areas of a given piece that could benefit from a completely new approach, and he is able to brainstorm and execute different approaches.

WHY IS THIS IMPORTANT?

In my experience, students struggle to mindfully do the hard work of W.CCR.5 simply because they don't see any great reason to do it. Sure, poorly edited papers may result in a lower grade or a paper that isn't accepted until revisions are made, but at the end of the day, school writing—unlike college or career writing—is often aimed at audiences students find inauthentic.

One response to this problem has been to give students wider audiences to write for, beyond simply the teacher or fellow students. Although this may seem progressive, we have to realize that, in the world of college and career, writing is most often viewed impartially and for its ability to do its core job of communicating something. Therefore, even if a writer can create vivid images or striking metaphors, it tends not to matter if she can't copyedit for surface errors and mechanics or bring a critical, impartial eye to her piece's ability to clearly and efficiently do what it was written to do. This is problematic considering that even the most authentic audiences for student writers will view student work with greater charity than the typical college or career reader.

Ultimately, we must help our students own the truth that, whether their assignment requires them to write for the teacher or their peers or a more nontraditional audience, they must keep their eyes not on how immediately fulfilling they find a given task or audience to be, but rather on the fact that, if they are on a mission to become effective, efficient editors and revisers of their own writing, every assignment is a chance to get better at editing and revising. The ability to do these things is the true secret of making good writing great.

W.CCR.

6

The 6th college and career readiness anchor standard within the writing strand of the CCSS reads as follows:

> Use technology, including the Internet, to produce and publish writing and to interact and collaborate with others.

Now then: how about we talk about technology and education?

"WE BOUGHT iPADS, AND NOW WE'RE COMMON CORE ALIGNED!"

I once heard a school leader claim her school was on its way to Common Core alignment because she had just purchased an iPad for every child in the building. I instantly facepalmed on hearing this, because Common Core alignment, as I hope you're learning through this book, isn't about buying

iPads. In fact, an iPad alone does *nothing* to increase one's likelihood of being college and career ready. Conversely, when technology (iPads or otherwise) is integrated thoughtfully and efficiently, it can promote college and career readiness.

Although the computer-based tests of the Smarter Balanced Assessment Consortium and the Partnership for Assessment of Readiness for College and Careers are causing some districts to spend more on technology, I'd like to bury any lingering misconceptions you may have about the Common Core's technology emphasis. In fact, there is no such emphasis, with very few anchor standards explicitly mentioning technology. I count only three:

- W.CCR.6—See earlier.

- W.CCR.8—"Gather relevant information from multiple print and **digital** sources..."

- SL.CCR.5—"Make strategic use of **digital** media and visual displays of data..."

This isn't to say that the Common Core intends for students to use technology with exceeding rarity—technology can be used to support mastery of every one of the 32 anchor standards, after all—but rather that 1:1 classrooms—that is, classrooms where every student has a computing device—aren't a prerequisite for Common Core success, and that when technology is used, it should be done thoughtfully and efficiently.[1]

With all of that said, let's explore the techiest anchor standard in the Common Core, which is all about leveraging technology to produce and publish writing.

PRODUCE AND PUBLISH WRITING WITH TECHNOLOGY

I'm glad this standard is in the Common Core. I'm pretty old school when it comes to literacy, but there's no doubt that college- and career-ready people are aware of the powerful amplifying effect technology can have on a writer's work. Today anyone with the grit to learn how to use an online publishing platform—like WordPress, for example, on which I build my blog—can literally write things for the whole world to read. (If it weren't for online publishing, you wouldn't be holding this book.)

To help students prepare to use technology at a college- and career-ready level, they need ample experience thinking through the implications of, and practicing the strategies and methods for, producing and publishing writing online. Having a sophisticated awareness of what it means to post something—on social media or on a blog or anywhere else—can help students with everything from getting a job to creating a company of their own.

At the time of this writing, a person needs only an Internet connection and a Web browser to access everything from word processing software (for example, Google Docs) to the top publication platforms (for example,

---

1. As some will point out, although the Common Core may not mandate technology acquisition, the assessments being created to hold schools accountable for Common Core mastery are computer based, thus requiring schools to pony up for tech updates. This is true, and I've purposefully avoided talk of the CCSS-aligned standardized tests in this book because, frankly, the standardized testing conversation in the United States makes the Common Core conversation seem tame. I'm not going there—I'm a teacher, not a standardized test prepper; no test will ever change that. With all that being said, I maintain that technology access isn't a *prerequisite* for Common Core success.

WordPress, Tumblr, Weebly)—and all of this is free. Essentially, all the tools for writing for huge audiences have been democratized to the extent that all that stands between a person and millions of readers is the skill—and certainly the business savvy—of the writer.

With that being said, it must be emphasized that simply requiring kids to keep a blog or use Google Docs won't guarantee their success in college or career, and in fact can be an enormous waste of time. It is much more critical, really, that they be able to write well. In other words, they must master the other writing anchor standards. In a way, W.CCR.6 is the rocket that propels a ship into space: it's not the ship itself, but rather a means of getting the ship to its destination.

AN ILLUSTRATIVE ANECDOTE

As a member of the high school graduating class of 2002, the snazziest technology I could access in elementary school was the occasional game of Frogger on a classroom Macintosh. By the time I graduated from high school, Microsoft's Hotmail was just coming into vogue, AOL Instant Messenger was the coolest thing I could do on my home's dial-up Internet connection, and "Web 2.0" was still a nerd-only word.

Yet, when Facebook came out, I figured out how to use it. Slowly but surely, I figured out that there were things that should be posted and things that shouldn't. When blogs became accessible via Blogger and WordPress, I began to dabble in them—not because a teacher told me to, but because I saw them as an opportunity to share my writing. Through using them, I figured them out.

In terms of the technology instruction I received in my K–12 education, I had a keyboarding course in middle school (and thank you, Mr. Nash, for strictly enforcing the "don't look at your fingers" rule); a Microsoft Office class as a high school freshman; and a computer science course in which I learned Visual Basic computer language. All of these classes, looking back, were great at developing in me a critical physical skill (keyboarding) and thinking abilities (by showing me how computer software features tend to be organized and how computers run on code). In all of my other courses, we rarely used technology except for writing papers.

And despite not having spent countless hours in my core classes using the latest technology, I have graduated from a demanding university, found employment wherever I've moved, and altogether flourished in the twenty-first-century world that has come of age along with me.

To what do I credit my success? I lack much innate talent or intelligence. Rather, I was given a boatload of reading, writing, thinking, speaking, and character instruction. In anchor standard terms, I was made college and career ready in all of the other anchor standards, and this made W.CCR.6 a cinch.

Now, with all that being said, I do think W.CCR.6 prompts us to think of ways to incorporate more technology into our writing instruction, especially when it comes to producing and publishing writing.

Producing Writing

For producing writing, I still think Microsoft Word is an essential program. Alternative (and often free) programs like Google Docs and Open Office are getting better all the time, but Word, if your district can afford it, is still the quintessential word processor. According to Bill Coplin (2012, p. 52),

> Bill Gates is the man behind Microsoft and, whether we love or despise him, we all need to thank him for Microsoft Word, which is the only word-processing tool you need to master. Other word-processing programs, no matter how cheap or quaint, are useless in writing for work. Most of you already know that and have some experience using Word. The rest of you need to get on board.

These words may seem strong, but, for at least the time being, they seem likely to remain true. Of the attachments I receive from teachers, publishers, and businesspeople through email, the vast majority are either in Microsoft Word format or in a PDF format produced with Microsoft Word.

Publishing Writing

Online platforms for publishing writing seem to multiply by the day. For the sake of getting the biggest bang for your time investment, it seems wise, if you're allowing students to publish pieces online, to teach them to use platforms that have been around for quite a while and seem set to stay. It's impossible to predict with absolute certainty which platforms will still be here in ten years, but, for my money, I would bet that WordPress will remain a top blogging platform for years to come. WordPress actually has an education-specific platform, too—check it out at http://edublogs.org.

INTERACT AND COLLABORATE WITH OTHERS THROUGH TECHNOLOGY

Perhaps one of the most powerful features of technology-based writing is the ability to interact and collaborate with people on a scale never seen before in history. I'll share a few of the modes of tech-based interaction and collaboration that college- and career-ready folks should be aware of.

First of all, email communication know-how is a must in the twenty-first century. Handwriting may be on its way to becoming a thing of the past, but it's likely that email is here to stay for as long as there's the Internet. More schools are looking to companies like Google to provide email accounts for all

of their students; in schools where this isn't possible, students should be encouraged to create professional email addresses as soon as they can (in other words, jonsmith@gmail.com instead of footballplayer1234@gmail.com), and to use them at least periodically to communicate with teachers.

When my freshman students interact with me through email, I tell them to pretend I am their future professor or boss. Many of them smile and nod, and then proceed to send me emails with vague, text-ish subject lines like "i need help" or messages like "hey stu, i turned in the arcle [sic] of the week." Whenever student emails are written in a way that is likely to decrease their standing in the eyes of an employer or professor, I simply respond with: "Dear So-and-So, Please reread your email and revise it to professional standards." In general, students are underprepared to treat online communication with the same care they should afford polished essays. Students should also know how to do basic tasks with email, like attach files (most of my students can do this) or insert links (most of my students need to be taught how to do this).

College- and career-ready people are also aware of the power and proper use of social media. Companies like Facebook, Twitter, and Instagram boast enormous memberships (Facebook now famously exceeds one billion users), and as a result they provide enormous potential for collaboration and interaction. However, content posted to these platforms is becoming increasingly scrutinized by college admissions officers, employers, and even lending institutions. In addition to that, interacting with peers via Facebook is rarely the best way to build one's communicative skills; also, it can become quite addicting. As a result, college- and career-ready people think critically about their use of social media and use it wisely.

College- and career-ready people should be aware of the relative ease with which they can work with others on a piece of writing, in real time; a platform for this collaboration that is becoming increasingly common in the realms of both business and education is Google Docs, which allows users to create a document; share it with peers; and work on the document together, through separate devices, in real time. In my own district, teachers are using this simple, powerful tool to create living, collaborative documents (for example, vertical curriculum progressions), and students are using Google Docs for everything from lab reports to group presentations.

WHY IS THIS IMPORTANT?

Though it's becoming increasingly rare, I still have students ask me if they can just handwrite an assignment instead of doing it digitally. The old school in me respects their no-frills instincts, but few careers currently exist in which some form of digital writing or collaboration isn't called for, and that number seems destined only to shrink with time. Consequently, I like to inspire students to consider just what's possible if they become excellent writers who know how to use technology strategically, and toward that end I love showing them examples of people who have created online businesses for themselves.

One example I share with students is Pat Flynn. Pat, as his readers know him, was an architect studying for an industry test when he decided to put his notes online in the form of a blog. His goal was to learn the content for the test more deeply by writing about what he was learning in a manner that was useful for others. When Pat was laid off from his job several years into his blogging, however, he realized that the large audience he had developed would be likely to appreciate a polished, portable ebook of his best material. He created a simple PDF study guide that quickly sold well enough to support his family, and ever since he has been experimenting with different forms of online income and writing about it on his *Smart Passive Income Blog* (www.smartpassiveincome.com).

Pat's story is one of insane success—he now averages an income of $50,000 per *month*—but I share it with my students because, for many of them, this type of entrepreneurship helps motivate them not just to get good at using technology strategically, but, even more important, to become great written communicators.

The 7th college and career readiness anchor standard within the writing strand of the CCSS reads as follows:

> Conduct short as well as more sustained research projects based on focused questions, demonstrating understanding of the subject under investigation.

This standard is part of the trio of "Research to Build and Present Knowledge" anchor standards (W.CCR.7–9). All of these standards involve using a source to learn something new, and then sharing that new learning with an audience. Understanding that as the overlapping theme of the three anchors, in my discussions of them I'll focus on the aspects that make them unique. In the case of W.CCR.7, there are three skills to consider.

CONDUCT RESEARCH PROJECTS OF VARYING LENGTH

College- and career-ready people see research, like so many skills within the Common Core, less as an isolated project or assignment and more as an intellectual habit. As a result, they think of research strategically, widening or narrowing the scope of their inquiry on an as-needed basis.

From an instructional standpoint, teachers should rejoice at this standard's equal emphasis on both short and sustained research projects. This means our units of study, whether in science or history or English, can incorporate research tasks without requiring days spent in the computer lab. The short research task can be completed in as little as a class period; for example, prior to a field trip to a local university's engineering fair, my students spend a class period researching various fields of engineering in preparation for the questions they'll be expected to ask the college students we'll be meeting the next day.

FOCUS YOUR RESEARCH QUESTIONS

The foundation of an effective research project, whether it's long or short, is a focused question. I have been the knucklehead who assigns an open-ended, self-generated research project with way too little guidance. I thought I was awesome: kids were going to get to research something they were genuinely interested in. The problem is, without at least guiding them in the development of focused and intriguing research questions, I have also been the poor sap with a stack of papers "about" global warming or abortion or animal abuse. Sadly, such unfocused papers aren't just unpleasant to read, they are also needlessly frustrating to write. Even when students choose their topics, research bores and serves little purpose if it doesn't answer an interesting and focused question.

For those self-guided research projects I just mentioned, how fascinating would it have been if my students and I

had worked on refining their "topics" into narrow, focused questions? Here are some possibilities derived from the examples just given:

- Which people or groups call global warming a hoax, and which call it a reality? What commonalities exist among these opposing camps? What evidence do these groups use to support their arguments?

- Give an overview of the spectrum of actions that pro-life and pro-choice groups have taken to advance their respective causes. In your opinion, and based on your reading of the Constitution, which of these actions are acceptable in the United States of America?

- How have animal rights advocates affected the incidence of animal abuse cases? What factors might skew your findings?

This standard does not limit itself to self-generated research questions, and so teachers have to become excellent at creating focused questions within their units of study. Here are some research questions more germane to my task as a world history and English teacher:

- For *All Quiet on the Western Front* (Remarque, 1929) and our 1900–1950 world history unit: What impact does war have on soldiers?

Research a war from the twentieth century, explain the war's causes and effects, and discuss whether the impact on soldiers was worth the results of the war.

- For *Things Fall Apart* (Achebe, 1959) and our world history unit on the 1800s: Was Africa a land devoid of civilization prior to the imperialism of the nineteenth and twentieth centuries? Chinua Achebe's *Things Fall Apart* offers an emphatic "No," but what other evidence can you find to support Achebe's implied assertions? After sharing your findings, explain to your reader how Africa should be viewed today by people in our small town.

- For a world history unit spanning the years from 1950 to today: The North Korean political prisons are the longest-running concentration camps in at least the last one hundred years. Why does the world allow them to exist? Seek an answer to this question as well as one self-generated question as you research one group that is working to free North Korea's political prisoners.

All of these would be extended research projects, but with some tweaking they could be focused down into shorter projects as well.

DEMONSTRATE NEWFOUND UNDERSTANDINGS

The most nuanced part of this standard is demonstrating one's newfound understandings. College and career readiness doesn't mean writing a research paper in which you introduce your topic at the beginning and then use a paragraph for each source you explored, summarizing that source's contents. Rather, this standard envisions a paper that explores the focused question or problem that prompted the research, with information gained in research integrated "selectively," not exhaustively, for the sake of "maintain[ing] the flow of ideas" (W.9–10.8) in a way that demonstrates that you really understand the topic. In other words, college- and career-ready research is done not to create a summary of the research, but rather to undergird one's writing.

WHY IS THIS IMPORTANT?

Few employers or professors will want a summary of findings on broad, unfocused topics. In the information age, the ability to efficiently answer questions and solve problems using research will be invaluable. This skill set is valuable even in one's personal life: the Internet provides helpful solutions to everything from how to fix the garbage disposal to how to potty train a toddler, yet these solutions aren't accessible to those without the intellectual habits laid out in this standard.

The 8th college and career readiness anchor standard within the writing strand of the CCSS reads as follows:

> Gather relevant information from multiple print and digital sources, assess the credibility and accuracy of each source, and integrate the information while avoiding plagiarism.

This standard is the second part of the research writing trio of anchor standards (W.CCR.7–9). Because the three somewhat overlap, I'll again only touch on aspects of W.CCR.8 that make it unique.

GATHER RELEVANT INFO FROM MULTIPLE SOURCES

College- and career-ready people think strategically about where they will gather information for a research task. Their question (W.CCR.7) naturally informs the types of sources they will seek, and they then go about the task of searching for those source types. Here are some questions we can explore with our students around the task of gathering information:

- How do we gather information on a question from multiple sources?

- What's the point of using multiple sources when we're pursuing a research question?

- How do we find information that is relevant to our research question?

- What can we do if our first Google search doesn't result in the kind of information we are looking for?

- How do we organize useful information as we come across it? In other words, how do we gather it?

HOW DO SEARCH ENGINES LIKE GOOGLE WORK?

This is a bit nerdy, but my ninth-grade students take an interest in it. Basically, few people are totally sure how Google ranks its search results (Google's algorithm is its golden goose, you could say), but we know the algorithm seeks to determine a site's authority and relevance for a given query, looking at factors like how long a site has been around, how many indexed pages it has, how many other sites link to the site, and how frequently the site uses whatever words you're searching for. With that being said, there's a lot to be gained by having a website that can rank high in Google, so an entire industry of search engine optimization experts and programs has developed, constantly seeking to figure out how to get on the coveted first page of a Google search for a given high-volume keyword. As a result, there are times when sites that are high on the list are actually not that reliable at all.

ASSESS THE CREDIBILITY AND ACCURACY OF SOURCES

Credibility, I tell my students, should remind them of the word "incredible." If something is credible, it is believable, so if something is *in*credible, it is unbelievable. I make the related point that when we are doing research, we have to train a little sensor in our brain that detects a given source's level of credibility. I then ask my students what this "sensor" should look for to determine credibility, and they quickly come up with a list of things like how recently the source was written, how professionally it is presented, who wrote it, and so on.

Accuracy is closely linked to credibility; to help my students grasp accuracy, I ask them what it would mean if I said I was an accurate three-point shooter (at which they invariably laugh). It would mean, they say, that I tend to put the ball in the hoop when I shoot it from beyond the three-point arc. For something to be accurate, I say, it must hit the mark—the basketball shot must land precisely where it was intended to land. When researching, we want to ensure that our sources are accurately representing the things they claim to represent. On the one hand, if we are only using a source as a method for building general knowledge on a topic, accuracy isn't something we need to obsess over; on the other hand, if we are using a source to support an argument we are building or to help prove our hypothesis, we had better try to confirm the source's accuracy with another source, especially if the source we're considering doesn't seem perfectly credible.

INTEGRATE INFORMATION WITHOUT PLAGIARIZING

Here's where pen meets paper in W.CCR.8. College- and career-ready people must be able to take the information they've gathered and vetted and incorporate it into pieces of writing or presentations without plagiarizing. I tell my students that the most effective writers and thinkers on the planet constantly use the words of others in their writing, but they always put quotation marks around these words and cite the sources from which they came. It is *not* plagiarism to do this, but it *is* plagiarism to use someone else's ideas or words without giving that person proper credit. To add nuance to this concept, I bring up the idea of fair use, which often intrigues students; for example, it's not okay to quote large chunks of an author's work or to merely augment a string of quotes from an author with minimal text. In all situations in which a writer uses another author's work, there are agreed-on formats for citing that work (MLA and APA are two of the most prominent); students ready for college and career know how to use the Internet to look up the specific requirements for these formats.

WHY IS THIS IMPORTANT?

The ever-expanding breadth of the Internet will only continue to increase the importance of the skills in this standard. It is the world's information garbage dump *and* the world's information gold mine, but many lack the skills needed to determine the trash from the treasure. College- and career-ready people do have these skills, and as a result they are able to quickly and efficiently gather information from diverse and credible sources, coming up with ideas and solutions that are entirely new. Our students must become excellent at these skills if they are to make themselves valuable to employers in a world as quickly changing as ours.

The 9th college and career readiness anchor standard within the writing strand of the CCSS reads as follows:

> Draw evidence from literary or informational texts to support analysis, reflection, and research.

This is the final element of the research writing trio of anchor standards (W.CCR.7–9). It boils down to using other texts to strengthen and support our own writing—and I'm not just talking about arguments here.

BACK UP STUFF WITH EVIDENCE

Here are some questions I might ask my students in pursuit of mastering this standard:

- What is evidence?
- What's the difference between evidence and details or facts?
- What must evidence do?

Essentially, I want my students to see how rich writing can be when it is in conversation with other texts. Gerald Graff, former president of the Modern Language Association, developed this idea in his seminal work, *Clueless in Academe* (2003). Writing across the disciplines, Graff pointed out, is not a set of isolated papers, but rather a *network* of papers, all of which are in conversation with one another— sometimes arguing, sometimes explaining, sometimes narrating, yet always acting like a gigantic, growing, collaborative brain.

Using evidence in our writing, therefore, is consciously collaborating with other writers, intentionally building on what others have written. When my students and I are in tune with this, I see less "quote bombing" (that is, students' just picking out a quotation and including it in their piece because they are required to use a quotation) and more fluid, graceful thinking.

Here are some further questions I might ask to promote the awesomeness of evidence-based writing:

FOR ANALYSES

- How does this piece of the text support your theories? For example, how does Romeo's "But soft! What light through yonder window breaks?" line support or refute your idea that William Shakespeare (1992, 2.2.2) is portraying young love as foolish?

FOR REFLECTIONS

- Where in the text were you personally affected, emotionally or intellectually? Why do you think that is? What did the author do to influence you?

- What lines stood out to you? Why?

FOR RESEARCH

- How does this piece of quoted text add to the central idea or claim you're trying to communicate? Is it truly worth including? Why?

WHY IS THIS IMPORTANT?

In many workplaces and college classrooms, opinions and philosophies rule zero-sum conversations in which all parties are interested only in promoting their side. A robust understanding of evidence and the ability to procure it help fix this common malaise, allowing students and workers to push through philosophies to get close to the bottom of a matter. The people able to do this work—that is, who are able to find and use evidence effectively—quickly become thought leaders. It's not that they come up with the best-sounding ideas, but rather that they are able to habitually detect the difference between what sounds good and what is good.

10

(Wipes sweat from brow.) All right, let's finish these writing anchor standards. The 10th (and final!) college and career readiness anchor standard within the writing strand of the CCSS reads as follows:

> Write routinely over extended time frames (time for research, reflection, and revision) and shorter time frames (a single sitting or a day or two) for a range of tasks, purposes, and audiences.

Just as R.CCR.10, the reading anchor standard that calls for grade-appropriate text complexity, is a kind of overarching principle for all of the reading standards, so W.CCR.10 is for the writing standards.

WRITE LIKE CRAZY

The more we have students write, the more literacy skills they will develop—and this isn't limited to written literacy. In *Writing to Read: Evidence for How Writing Can Improve Reading* (Graham & Hebert, 2010), researchers share three findings that are highly relevant to this standard:

- When students write about the texts they read, their reading and writing improve.

- When students learn about and engage in the writing process behind creating texts, their reading and writing improve.

- When students write their own texts frequently, their reading and writing improve.

This is all great news, but asking students to write routinely—literally as part of a class's daily normal functioning—is only possible if teachers think smarter about assessing and giving feedback on student writing. Students need to write vastly more than any one teacher can read, and the only way they can do that is if we view writing as a learning process as well as a product-oriented task. A classroom in which students will grow in this standard quickly is one in which students are writing everything from quickwrites to process-written, formal papers.

WRITE FOR LOTS OF TAPS

Remember TAP from W.CCR.4? A key to getting students writing all the time is thinking broadly about the different tasks, audiences, and purposes our students can write for. The only requirement, really, is that students have a balanced and generous diet of writing.

So, in writing about texts, students could write…

- Personal reactions
- Analyses
- Interpretations
- Arguments
- Summaries
- Notes
- Questions
- Answers

In other words, students should respond to texts with pieces long and short, formal and informal, night and day.

And in practicing writing apart from texts, students could write…

- Short stories
- Autobiographies or biographies
- Poems
- Essays
- Op-eds
- How-to articles
- Wiki contributions
- Blog posts

…and just about anything else you can think of. A key consideration for schools will be how to get students writing frequently while also providing a coherent increase in complexity and challenge as students advance toward graduation.

WHY IS THIS IMPORTANT?

Fostering the ability to write well is not a matter of throwing in a standards-based lesson or assignment every now and then; rather, it will require the frequency of writing called for in this standard. When students ask why so much writing is necessary, they need to know that writing "appears to be a 'marker' attribute of high-skill, high-wage, professional work"

(National Commission on Writing for America's Families, Schools, and Colleges, 2004, p. 19), and therefore it's a skill all of our students need and should want to have in their back pocket.

I like to tell my students that the Navy SEALs are some of the most adaptable military units in the world because of the intense training they undergo. When SEALs are given a task anywhere in the world, they tend to succeed regardless of the environment. I tell my students that writing is as critical for the adaptable, successful person of the twenty-first century as the ability to swim is for a Navy SEAL. With that in mind, we must seek to instill in our students the same sense of ownership of their writing skills that SEALs have for their swimming skills.

PART IV

The Anchor Standards in Speaking and Listening

ONCE YOU'VE PAGED THROUGH THE WRITING STRAND OF THE ANCHOR STANDARDS, you'll find the anchor standards in speaking and listening. The question these anchor standards seek to answer is, What should a college- and career-ready person be able to do as a speaker and listener?

HOW ARE THE ANCHOR STANDARDS IN SPEAKING AND LISTENING ORGANIZED?

There are only 6 speaking and listening standards, and they are broken up into 2 groups:

1. Comprehension and Collaboration (SL.CCR.1–3)

2. Presentation of Knowledge and Ideas (SL.CCR.4–6)

Or, in everyday human terms, these anchor standards are dedicated to answering these questions:

1. How do you prepare for and effectively participate in a range of conversations and collaborations with diverse partners? How do you build on others' ideas and express your own clearly and persuasively? Can you integrate and evaluate information from a variety of sources? Can you evaluate a speaker's point of view, reasoning, and use of evidence and rhetoric?

2. Are you able to present information, findings, and supporting evidence in a way that allows your listeners to follow your line of reasoning? Are you strategic when you make visual displays to complement your speaking? Can you use formal English when appropriate?

All in all, speaking and listening are skills that too often get ignored, but few abilities are as crucial as the ones contained within this strand. Students need and love to have ample opportunity to take part in a variety of rich, structured conversations. They need practice doing this in pairs, in small groups, and as a whole class. We need to find ways to ensure that they are productive members of the conversations we ask them to take part in, and methods for holding them accountable and giving them descriptive feedback range from attentively circulating through the classroom during small-group discussions to using a rubric to assess student speaking skills in a whole-class debate.

The 1st college and career readiness anchor standard within the speaking and listening strand of the Common Core State Standards (CCSS) reads as follows:

> Prepare for and participate effectively in a range of conversations and collaborations with diverse partners, building on others' ideas and expressing their own clearly and persuasively.

Let's play talk to the teacher!

On second thought, let's not. It's far too common in classrooms to witness large groups of students taking turns speaking to the instructor. And although this is one mode of speaking that students must be adept at, college- and career-ready people also need to be able to flourish in the much more frequent modes of one-on-one and small-group discussions. When reading the specific anchor skills that follow, keep in mind

that they are pertinent for a variety of conversation types.

COME TO CONVERSATIONS PREPARED

SL.CCR.1 basically says, "The most productive members of conversations begin by being prepared." This may mean reading the homework, doing the practice problem, completing the quickwrite, reading independently in pursuit of one's own interests, or taking notes on the lecture. In essence, we're alluding to a phenomenon everyone has experienced: the more knowledgeable a person is on a topic, the more ready she is to participate in discussions on it.

Discussions around texts are particularly useful for practicing this skill. When we give students time to closely read and annotate a text in preparation for a discussion around a given topic or set of broad, open-ended questions, we are giving them a chance to prepare what they will say. Such work makes close reading and annotation a task connected with an authentic outcome—in this case, a discussion around a text—and therefore students are likely to undertake the preparation with greater vigor.

CONVERSE EFFECTIVELY WITH ANYONE ON THE PLANET

I'm glad this standard mentions "diverse partners," because the college- and career-ready person certainly needs to know how to work with all kinds of people. At the most basic level, this means being socially intelligent enough to detect when you are bothering someone and to predict which kinds of comments or language choices may be offensive to a given audience. At a more advanced level, college- and career-ready people are able to engage in productive conversations with anyone, even people from vastly different settings. Practicing this work is more possible than ever thanks to the Internet. A colleague of mine, Erica Beaton, once demonstrated this masterfully by having her sophomores engage in an online chat with *New York Times* best-selling author

Malcolm Gladwell. This experience wasn't just "cool" for students; it also gave them experience conversing with someone quite different from them.

BUILD ON OTHERS' IDEAS AND CLEARLY, PERSUASIVELY EXPRESS YOUR OWN

Once students are prepared both for the topic under discussion and a diversity of people with whom to discuss it, they need to know how to speak productively in a conversation. Productive conversing hinges on two basic moves—hearing the ideas of others and building on them with your own.

Balancing these two moves is critical. If a person ignores the ideas of others and only expresses his own, he will frustrate himself and others with his apparent egocentrism; conversely, if a person is only able to parrot back the ideas of others without having (or at least expressing) any of his own, he will again frustrate himself and others with his apparent lack of anything to bring to the conversation. In contrast to both of these hypothetical people, an effective conversationalist listens to and builds on the ideas of others and expresses his own.

To help students master this balance, here are some key teaching moves that transcend disciplinary boundaries:

1. Explicitly teach students about the two conversational actions, and lead them to understand the importance of each.

2. Model the two moves daily, and be explicit with students when you are doing each.

3. Provide students with sentence templates (*They Say, I Say* [Graff & Birkenstein, 2014] offers an incredible variety) that give them an explicit sense of the type of language needed for each move. For example, "So-and-so, I hear you saying _____, to which I would add _____."

4. Provide students with opportunities to practice each kind of conversational move in isolation and in unison. For example, I usually have a conversation toward the beginning of the school year in which students can *only use* the template in the previous list item. This may seem likely to stunt their conversation, but I find that my students need more practice listening to and paraphrasing others for us to have beautiful conversations and debates later on in the school year.

5. Provide students with feedback on how they are doing. This can be done through tracking the specific moves they carry out in a conversation; training students to track specific moves used (this can be a rotating duty, allowing all students to gain some experience evaluating conversational moves); and even filming students and showing them clips after the conversation is through.

WHY IS THIS IMPORTANT?

Since I first began incorporating an abundance of in-class debates and discussions into my teaching several years ago, I've been amazed at how students have improved at talking not just *to* but *with* each other. This has been partly due to explicit instruction, partly due to frequent practice, and partly due to simply striving to model these two conversational moves as I speak with my students.

The reason why I am excited about my students' growth is that, when my students occasionally get the benefit of hearing guest speakers from businesses in the community, these people from the world of work constantly cite the ability to verbally communicate as critical for success and promotion in their respective areas of work. This means that teachers who dream of their students' flourishing in the long run must pay attention to the speaking and listening standards, and SL.CCR.1 in particular.

The 2nd college and career readiness anchor standard within the speaking and listening strand of the CCSS reads as follows:

> Integrate and evaluate information presented in diverse media and formats, including visually, quantitatively, and orally.

You'll probably notice that this standard somewhat echoes R.CCR.7 and W.CCR.8. The authors of the Common Core were clearly focused on the fact that, in a world of exponentially increasing information, the ability to evaluate and integrate information from any given knowledge source is critical. Here are the basic questions a college- and career-ready person can answer, according to this standard.

HOW DO I INTEGRATE INFORMATION FROM A GIVEN SOURCE?

Integration, remember, is the task of taking separate items and bringing them together into a coherent whole. In the case of this standard, we're talking about taking a given source and incorporating some or all of its key information into whatever argument or presentation or discussion we're working on or preparing for. Because there's so much information in most sources, the college- and career-ready person is choosy, knowing that he can't possibly capture every nugget of information he comes across.

Picture a first-year college student sitting in a lecture hall. This student must be adept at detecting and capturing the key points of the lecture. If she errs on the side of efficiency in her note taking but fails to bring the lecture's key points to bear in a discussion or an examination, she will struggle to succeed. At the same time, if she attempts to record every single item from the professor's lecture with no thought as to what information is most critical, she will probably struggle to integrate the lecture knowledge into her working memory.

The best way for instructors to help students grapple with knowledge integration tasks like this is to model how they themselves think through the process of integrating information—especially, for the sake of this standard, oral information. YouTube offers us a treasure trove of high-quality lectures and explanatory videos with which we can model our note-taking processes. For example, I often incorporate the Crash Course YouTube channel (www.youtube.com/user/crashcourse) into my units—these fast-paced, often humorous videos set the comprehension bar high in a growing number of subjects, including literature, history, science, and psychology. Another phenomenal (and enormous) resource is the expanding set of TED Talks (www.youtube.com/user/TED TalksDirector).

WHEN DO I INTEGRATE INFORMATION FROM A GIVEN SOURCE?

In the process of integrating information from diverse sources, college- and career-ready people habitually evaluate a source's reliability. Evaluation, I tell students, is determining a source's **value** for our current purposes: Is the source trustworthy (see R.CCR.7)? Is the information accurate? Is the information necessary? This final consideration of necessity is especially important when dealing with oral information sources, such as lectures. The best way to teach students to choose necessary information is, again, to have them listen to or watch some of the high-quality lectures available online. Have students take notes while they do this (and take notes along with them), perhaps pausing periodically to ask them to compare notes with you or with their peers (Burke, 2013).

Ultimately, this standard aims at using diverse information sources for powerful purposes. In SL.11–12.2, the purpose of the information integration we've been discussing is "to make informed decisions and solve problems." When a college- and career-ready person sees a problem in her world or place of work, she pursues solutions that may not even exist yet through effectively grappling with the enormous amounts of available information. My father, a director of operations at an international manufacturing company, always says that there are two kinds of people in the world: problem makers and problem solvers. He says that he is always looking for people who fall within the latter category, and that they tend to quickly rise through the ranks of the company. College- and career-ready people, as envisioned in this standard, are exactly the kinds of people my father and thousands like him are looking for.

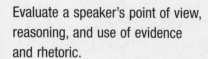

SL.CCR. 3

The 3rd college and career readiness anchor standard within the speaking and listening strand of the CCSS reads as follows:

> Evaluate a speaker's point of view, reasoning, and use of evidence and rhetoric.

This standard boils down to thinking critically about a speaker and his words. Should we listen to this person? Why or why not? A college- and career-ready person habitually evaluates the information she encounters. When listening to a speaker, there are several considerations a person would use for such an evaluation.

WHAT ARE THE STRENGTHS AND LIMITATIONS OF THIS SPEAKER'S POINT OF VIEW?

As we discussed in R.CCR.6, point of view is where a speaker is coming from. A helpful acronym for analyzing a speaker's point of view is "SOAPS" (Burke, 2013, p. 152):

- What is the **subject** of this speech?
- What is the **occasion** for this speech?
- Who is the **audience** for this speech?
- What is the **purpose** of this speech?
- Who is the **speaker**?

Few realms offer better examples of these kinds of determinations than politics. At the time of this writing, President Barack Obama's economic stimulus law has reached its five-year anniversary. As a result, all of the political players are currently talking about the legislation, albeit with vastly different takes on its effectiveness. President Obama and his supporters, on the one hand, speak positively of the law and its effects; Republicans, on the other hand, decry its wasteful-ness and impotence. When listening to speeches on this topic, considera-tions of the speaker's point of view are a critical starting point for evaluation.

WHAT ARE THE STRENGTHS AND LIMITATIONS OF THIS SPEAKER'S USE OF EVIDENCE AND REASONING?

It does us little good to give a speaker's point of view too much power in our evaluation of a speech. For example, there are many who, simply because a speech comes from a political party they despise, immediately evaluate the speech as worthless and wrong based on point of view alone. College- and

career-ready people are not so quick to draw conclusions, instead drilling down deeper into a speaker's use of evidence and reasoning.

When grappling with evidence, here are some questions college- and career-ready people consider:

- What debatable claims does the speaker present? Are these supported with evidence?

- Does the speaker cite reputable sources when giving evidence?

- Is the speaker's evidence legitimately connected to what she is saying?

This last question leads into reason-ing, which is the glue that connects one's evidence to one's point; drawing on our knowledge of arguments from W.CCR.1, this is the warrant. Here are some questions college- and career-ready people ask when considering a speaker's reasoning:

- Is the speaker satisfactorily explain-ing how her evidence supports her claims?

- Is the speaker making logical points that come together to form a coher-ent whole?

- Is the speaker making any unsup-ported assumptions?

- What does the speaker *not* explain? Why might that be?

WHAT ARE THE STRENGTHS AND LIMITATIONS OF THIS SPEAKER'S USE OF RHETORIC?

Rhetoric, I explain to my students, is the artistic side of speaking. It involves the use of techniques aimed at influencing the audience's thoughts, emotions, and actions. Again, here are some questions for considering a speaker's use of rhetoric:

- Is the speaker trying to appeal to something besides my logic?

- Is he trying to make me feel strong, logic-impairing emotions like fear, guilt, or anger?

- To what extent does the speech seem to rely on my emotional response?

WHY IS THIS IMPORTANT?

The past century's wars and genocides have shown us the incredible, destructive power a speaker can have on a populace unable to objectively evaluate what they hear. In our earliest debates, I often see my students naturally resorting to rhetoric rather than reason, offering speeches replete with unexplained and usually unconscious assumptions. Sadly, this is not an area of weakness for teenagers alone: it riddles all rungs and sectors of society. The good news in this dreary picture, however, is that college- and career-ready people are able, first, to see speeches objectively, and, second, to produce speeches that have an uncanny power to connect with audiences that stems from their intentional use of evidence, reasoning, and rhetoric.

The 4th college and career readiness anchor standard within the speaking and listening strand of the CCSS reads as follows:

> Present information, findings, and supporting evidence such that listeners can follow the line of reasoning and the organization, development, and style are appropriate to task, purpose, and audience.

SL.CCR.1 focused on participating in conversations of various types, whereas this standard is about getting in front of people and speaking effectively, largely thanks to an internalized understanding of our old friend TAP (task, audience, and purpose).

BEGIN WITH TAP

Great speakers use TAP to determine how to prepare for and deliver an effective presentation. Realistically considering TAP is freeing because it allows us to get rid of delusions of grandeur. If I may draw from personal experience, in 2013 I was given the daunting task of delivering our school's commencement address, and although I was initially flattered, I quickly became paralyzed by my illogical thinking about TAP in this situation. In my mind, my task was to provide the best speech my audience had ever heard, my audience was every single one of the two thousand or so people who would attend graduation, and my purpose was to improve the trajectory of the graduates' lives. Talk about delusions of grandeur! Thankfully, in these times of paralysis my wife patiently reminded me that my task was, in fact, to give a pleasant, possibly moving, ten-minute speech; my audience was only the two hundred or so graduates who had chosen me for this honor (and many of these teenagers were kids I had previously taught); and my purpose was to get them thinking on one or two key points that had helped me in my postsecondary life.

That was it. Ten minutes, two hundred teenagers, one to two things to think about. As a result of this much saner TAP, I was able to deliver a speech that mostly achieved what it was meant to do.

Steve Vree, a science teacher in our building, does a great job preparing his sophomore biology students for this standard by providing a capstone presentation challenge for them. Students are tasked with creating experiments from scratch and presenting their methods and results to local businesspeople. Vree has already given them a task, so he helps students think through audience and purpose with questions like the following:

- Given that your audience consists of businesspeople of a variety of ages, what knowledge can you assume they will bring to your presentation, and what knowledge will they lack that you will need to fill in for them?

- When members of the audience have experienced your presentation, what do you hope they will have learned? Be picky and focus on one to two outcomes.

CREATE A PRESENTATION THAT LISTENERS CAN FOLLOW

With the liberating insights gained from considering TAP, a college- and career-ready person is prepared to delve into intentionally crafting an effective presentation. For any given presentation, one must consider what to include (content) and how to include it (organization, development, and style).

Intentionally Selected Content

When determining what information, evidence, and findings to include, a speaker puts herself in her audience's place. She habitually asks herself questions like the following, and as a result her presentations are easy to follow:

- What pieces of content will be necessary to help my audience arrive at the understandings I intend?

- What claims am I making in this presentation, and with what specific pieces of evidence am I supporting them?

- Is this particular piece of content distracting from this presentation's primary purpose? Even though this data point may be intriguing, is it necessary for this particular speaking task?

- Are there ways in which I can simplify this content using visual aids? (See SL.CCR.5 for more information.)

Intentionally Selected Organization, Development, and Style

Although the content of a speech is critical, it will not find residence in a listener's mind if it is not organized and developed clearly and delivered in an appropriate style. Effectively organized presentations use signal phrases (for example, "First," "Second," "Third"; Erik Palmer [2011, p. 41] calls these "signposts") and verbal cues (for example, "In this presentation we'll be examining the last quarter's sales figures, then I'll present the likely causes of those numbers, and finally I'll end with three action steps that will take our company to our next set of sales goals").

Development "refers to the examples, ideas, details, and commentary the speaker adds to ensure the ideas are thoroughly expressed and effectively delivered, anticipating and responding to any questions the audience might have" (Burke, 2013, p. 160). In other words, when considering the development of a presentation, speakers ask themselves the following questions:

- What analogies or examples can I use to transform an abstract concept into more concrete language?

- Where in this presentation is my audience likely to become confused, and how can I efficiently deal with that confusion?

- Where in my presentation is the content quickly accessible for my audience, therefore needing less development than less accessible spots?

Finally, the style of a presentation should be appropriate for one's audience. When I am presenting to my colleagues at a department meeting, I am going to speak informally and in a down-to-earth manner, because anything otherwise would be incongruent with how our group normally operates. In contrast, when I present an idea to my principals, I am likely to adopt a more formal style. In both of these examples, I am adjusting my style to make my presentation easier to follow for my listeners; I'm trying to get "me" closely aligned with "them" so that they'll focus less on me or more on the ideas I'm seeking to communicate.

HOW SL.CCR.4 CAN SAVE THE WORLD

Scott Harrison is one example from the group of people today who are using SL.CCR.4 and the Internet to save the world—in Harrison's case, one clean water project at a time. Harrison wanted to present information about the water crisis (his task) to people who could do something about it (his audience). His purpose in doing this was to motivate people to make a contribution of any dollar amount toward creating universal access to clean water for the world's one billion or so people who lacked it.

To do this, Harrison dropped every preconception about how this kind of thing should be done. He knew that his audience had a diminishing attention span, and so he wanted his message and his call to action to be simple enough to tweet. Toward this end, Harrison founded Charity: Water. From the organization's name to its promotional materials to its funding allocation principles (100 percent of public donations go to the field; administrative costs are funded by a select group of private "angel" donors), Charity: Water maintains a simple and direct message and call to action. Essentially, Harrison needed to present the water crisis to a tech-connected and skeptical millennial generation. To do this, he made some major design changes to the concept of a charity.

As a result of Harrison's unintentional internalization of the skills in SL.CCR.4, Charity: Water, at the time of this writing, has provided clean water to 3.3 million people around the world. Remarkably, this has all been accomplished in only seven years.

WHY IS THIS IMPORTANT?

There are very few employment sectors where the ability to present effectively isn't highly valuable and promotion friendly. My brother-in-law recently began working at a new company, and he made an observation to me the other day that transfers well to most college and career settings: "My bosses don't want opinions on labor issues from a new guy like me; they want quick and easy-to-follow reports and commentary." In other words, employers want people who are deeply aware of the communicative task in front of them and who tackle that task with efficiency and effectiveness.

5

The 5th college and career readiness anchor standard within the speaking and listening strand of the CCSS reads as follows:

> Make strategic use of digital media and visual displays of data to express information and enhance understanding of presentations.

In other words, how do we leverage presentation supplements to increase the effectiveness of our presentations?

STRATEGIC USE . . .

The most important word in this standard is "strategic." For years, students have been creating slide shows with nifty animations—but for what purpose? In the world of college and career, presentations don't get points for being "nifty"—they get points for being effective. This means that the college- and career-ready person uses digital media and visual aids not for the sake of making something pretty or fun, but for the sake of enhancing information's accessibility or keeping audience members focused and engaged. Every last visual element is chosen with a purpose—to make the presentation clearer, more concrete, more comprehensible, or even more impressive.

. . . OF DIGITAL MEDIA AND VISUAL DISPLAYS OF DATA

With the word "strategic" planted firmly in the center of our attention, we can turn to the abundance of digital media and visual displays available to the modern presenter. For the sake of our general level of conversation here, I've provided some tips you as a teacher might employ in helping students practice the strategic use of digital media and visual displays.

- Show students examples of well-designed slides and poorly designed ones. For example, show slides that contain too much text, slides that contain low-resolution images, slides that use the nifty animation and sound effects of the nineties, and slides that use zany fonts. Compare these to the slides used in a TED Talk (www.youtube.com/user/TED talksDirector). Discuss with your students the supporting role that design plays in an effective presentation.

- Walk students through the basic components of a variety of presentation software—Google Presentation and Prezi are free and online; Microsoft's PowerPoint and Apple's Keynote tend to be attached to their respective operating systems—and allow them to choose one with which to create a presentation for a given assignment. Learning one platform's mechanics builds a knowledge base that transfers well to other platforms.

- Challenge students to create visual representations (graphs, charts, infographics, diagrams, images, and so on) of information they are seeking to present; help them realize that the slides are something for the audience to look at while listening to a speaker rather than something to read while ignoring him.

HOW SL.CCR.5 CAN SAVE THE WORLD, TOO

In SL.CCR.4, I profiled Scott Harrison and his work with Charity: Water; I'd like to expand on that profile by highlighting a powerful promotional video Charity: Water uses to educate and empower viewers to do something about the water crisis.[1] I show this video to my students as an exemplar of how digital media and visual displays can be used to *strategically* express information. In the space of less than three and a half minutes, the video incorporates visual storytelling, numbers, data, voice, and music, as well as SL.CCR.4 elements like organized information and rhetoric, both to inform viewers and to evoke emotions of first sadness and then empowerment. When showing this video to my students, I point out the following:

- Notice how the statistics and proportions are graphically represented; the viewer never feels like he is being subjected to a series of data points, but this is exactly the kind of evidence used throughout the video.

- Notice the way that a funded water project's impact is displayed visually at the end of the film.

- Notice how, at the end of the video, you can summarize the social and economic effects of the current water crisis and the methods with which it can be solved. Compare your current ability to summarize these things with your ability prior to watching this film. How did the filmmakers achieve this change in such a short film?

- This video uses every visual display and every second strategically, and as a result, complex ideas and information are presented in a manner that enhances our comprehension of the water crisis. This video has now been viewed over one million times, and because of its power, many children's lives have been saved.

---

1. Here is a link to the "Water Changes Everything" video: http://youtube/BCHhwxvQqxg.

WHY IS THIS IMPORTANT?

This standard envisions people who can leverage digital media and visual displays of data for whatever communicative tasks, audiences, and purposes they encounter. Such people are college and career ready because, when given the chance to present, they bring a sophisticated awareness of how media can enhance the impact that their words have on an audience; they do not simply make something pretty to preoccupy the audience while they sit through another presentation. As a result, the impact of their work tends to match the goals with which they plan for and deliver it.

SL.CCR. 6

The 6th college and career readiness anchor standard within the speaking and listening strand of the CCSS reads as follows:

> Adapt speech to a variety of contexts and communicative tasks, demonstrating command of formal English when indicated or appropriate.

Are there any linguistics nerds out there? You'll like this one.

ADAPT FOR CONTEXT

At its broadest level, this anchor standard again draws on TAP. We want our students to use these three considerations—task, audience, and purpose—to determine how they should speak. For example, we want them to know that in a conversation with friends they can use generous amounts of slang, but in conversations with prospective employers they should completely avoid it. Similarly, although clichés or incorrect grammar may be used without remark in informal settings, they will probably prove a liability to us in settings in which our speech is being analyzed by listeners.

In linguistics, changing dialects based on context is called "code switching." It's when we either consciously or unconsciously change speech patterns for the sake of achieving communicative purposes. For example, if I am trying to build rapport with students, I find myself using some of their frequently used words, yet when I am seeking to connect with colleagues, I am unlikely to use student speech patterns unless I'm attempting humor.

DEMONSTRATE FORMAL ENGLISH WHEN APPROPRIATE

Although there are many beautiful dialects of English, there is a power-laden version of it that the Common Core refers to as "formal English." If you're wondering what specific grammatical and mechanical elements formal English entails, flip ahead to L.CCR.1. In terms of SL.CCR.6, however, college- and career-ready people know that in most college and career settings it is wise to use language devoid of informal English, which ranges from nonstandard grammar and vocabulary usage to things like clichés, colloquialisms, and slang.

WHY IS THIS IMPORTANT?

This is not about demeaning a student's home dialect; instead, it's about equipping students with the language spoken by those in power. If our students want to have lives in which they truly flourish, they will need the ability to use formal English fluently and with ease. If they are unable to do this, they are likely to become frustrated when in-class discussions don't lead to good marks from the professor, job interviews don't lead to job offers, and presentations don't lead to promotions.

PART V

The Anchor Standards in Language

Woo-Hoo!

Now on to the final set of anchor standards in the Common Core State Standards: the language standards. The question these anchor standards seek to answer is, What should a college- and career-ready person be able to do with language, particularly in terms of conventions and vocabulary?

HOW ARE THE ANCHOR STANDARDS IN LANGUAGE ORGANIZED?

Similar to the anchor standards in speaking and listening, there are 6 language anchor standards, and they are broken up into 3 groups:

1. Conventions of Standard English (L.CCR.1–2)

2. Knowledge of Language (L.CCR.3)

3. Vocabulary Acquisition and Use (L.CCR.4–6)

Or, in everyday human terms, these anchor standards are dedicated to answering these questions:

1. When needed, can you write and speak using the conventions of standard English grammar and usage? When needed, can you write with conventional capitalization, punctuation, and spelling?

2. Can you use language as a tool for conveying meaning effectively? In other words, can you use language well enough that the language gets out of the way and the ideas get communicated?

3. Do you recognize when words have multiple meanings? Can you clarify how a particular word is being used by an author or speaker? Are you able to make sense of figurative language and nuanced word meanings? Do you habitually acquire vocabulary when it is used by an author or speaker, and do you accurately use it in other contexts?

The language anchor standards make pure communication possible. Without them, our students will continuously run into frustration when they're trying to communicate something in college or in the workplace. Of all the strands of anchor standards, these are the least sexy but perhaps the most fundamental. Your students may be able to practice the skills in the other strands without having the language standards in place, but it's inarguable that these standards are necessary to afford students the greatest chance to flourish.

The 1st college and career readiness anchor standard within the language strand of the Common Core State Standards (CCSS) reads as follows:

> Demonstrate command of the conventions of standard English grammar and usage when writing or speaking.

This anchor is closely connected to the last one we examined, SL.CCR.6. SL.CCR.6 focused on knowing when and how to demonstrate a command of the conventions of standard English in speaking, whereas this standard focuses on a more general grasp of conventionality that can be applied to both writing and speaking.

A NOTE ON THE INTERTWINING NATURE OF L.CCR.1–3

The first three anchor standards within the language strand are tightly interdependent, with L.CCR.1 and L.CCR.2 focusing on the concrete elements of conventionality (grammar, usage, spelling, and mechanics) and L.CCR.3 focusing on using this understanding of conventionality to craft effective, stylistically intentional language. For the sake of conceptualizing the kinds of skills contained in these three anchors, here are some specific, grade-level examples of what those first three standards contain; keep in mind, however, that the specified grade levels are when the skills are introduced, and that the skills still need attention in later grades as students' language use matures.

L.CCR.1—GRAMMAR AND USAGE

- "Ensure subject-verb agreement" (L.3.1—that is, the 1st standard within the language strand for grade 3).

- "Ensure pronoun-antecedent agreement" (L.3.1).

- Avoid using "inappropriate fragments and run-ons" (L.4.1).

- "Correctly use [high-frequency homophones]" (L.4.1).

- "Recognize and correct inappropriate shifts in verb tense" (L.5.1).

- "Recognize and correct inappropriate shifts in pronoun number and person" (L.6.1).

- "Recognize and correct vague pronouns" and ambiguous antecedents (L.6.1).

- "Recognize variations from standard English" and "improve expression in conventional language" (L.6.1).

- "Place phrases and clauses in a sentence" (L.7.1).

- "Recogniz[e] and correct misplaced and dangling modifiers" (L.7.1).

- "Recognize and correct inappropriate shifts in verb voice and mood" (L.8.1).

- "Use parallel structure" (L.9–10.1).

L.CCR.2—MECHANICS AND SPELLING

- "Use punctuation to separate items in a series" (L.5.2).

- "Use punctuation (commas, parentheses, dashes) to set off nonrestrictive elements" (L.6.2).

L.CCR.3—MEANING AND STYLE

- "Choose words and phrases for effect" (L.3.3).

- "Choose words and phrases to convey ideas precisely" (L.4.3).

- "Choose punctuation for effect" (L.4.3).

- "Vary sentence patterns [to clarify] meaning, [to enhance] reader or listener interest, and [for] style" (L.6.3).

- "Maintain consistency in style and tone" (L.6.3).

- "Recogniz[e] and eliminat[e] wordiness, awkwardness, and redundancy" (L.7.3).[1]

---

1. For a full table of the Common Core's "language progressive skills," see www.corestandards.org /ELA-Literacy/L/language-progressive-skills.

GRAMMAR AND USAGE: THE FOCUS OF L.CCR.1

Now that we've developed a broad sense of which skills are contained where in the first half of the language strand, we can turn to what L.CCR.1 contains. This standard is specifically focused on grammar and usage, which essentially boil down to how words come together to form sentences and how this coming together should and shouldn't be done. For our purposes in this book, we won't look at the individual grammar and usage skills laid out in the grade-specific standards, but I would like to offer a few thoughts on how to make yours one of those exceptional classrooms in which students gain a stronger grasp on grammar and usage.

First of all, do not model for your students how to have a negative attitude toward grammar and usage. It has become commonplace for teachers to undermine the importance of knowing how words come together to form conventional sentences, but this must become unacceptable for those of us who wish to see our students thrive someday. I will not negate the fact that, especially at the college- and career-ready level laid out in the Common Core, grammar and usage can become abstract and challenging. For example, in the ninth- and tenth-grade band of L.CCR.1 (L.9–10.1), students are expected to "use various types of phrases (noun, verb, adjectival, adverbial, participial, prepositional, absolute) and clauses (independent, dependent, noun, relative, adverbial) to convey specific meanings and add variety and interest to writing and presentations," and I'll fully admit that these concepts aren't immediately intriguing. But as alluded to in L.9–10.1, a strong, internalized understanding of these concepts enables people to *be* both more easily understood when they communicate and more engaging. In short, these are not rules as much as they are tools for building a flourishing life. Withholding them from students is withholding something of value.

Many of us teachers probably avoid grammar instruction, however, because it is very challenging, and because our students often bring such negative preconceptions of grammar when they come to our class. We must overcome our own challenges with grammar by continually building our knowledge of how language functions and of how best to communicate with others. They may not represent the most enjoyable of reading selections, but even books like Lynne Truss's humorous *Eats, Shoots and*

Leaves: The Zero Tolerance Approach to Punctuation (2003) offer us an avenue to build on our knowledge of conventionality and—here's the key—share with our students that we are doing so.

I believe simply modeling for our students our own language learning will help them see grammar less as a set of rules and more as a set of tools.

WHY IS THIS IMPORTANT?

Ultimately, grammar and usage can be conceived of as oppressive rules or empowering tools, but I've noticed that they tend not to oppress those who wrestle with them to the point of mastery. As we'll see in L.CCR.3, there is all the wiggle room in the world for those who possess a strong grasp of conventionality—but just as the karate kid first needed to learn to "wax on, wax off" before he could become a great fighter, so must our students learn grammar and usage before becoming effective writers and speakers.

The 2nd college and career readiness anchor standard within the language strand of the CCSS reads as follows:

> Demonstrate command of the conventions of standard English capitalization, punctuation, and spelling when writing.

This anchor comes in and cleans up the three types of conventions not addressed in L.CCR.1: capitalization, punctuation, and spelling.

CAPITALIZE CORRECTLY

Prior to the trend of ignoring capitalization when texting, posting to social media, or writing informal emails to friends, students only had to struggle with determining whether a word was a specific label (in other words, a proper noun) or not. But because so much of our written communication today is quick and informal, students now must also grapple with deeply ingrained habits of noncapitalization. When I was a high school student at the turn of the millennium, I doubt many of my teachers dealt with the lowercase "i," as in, "i like green eggs and ham," but now it is one of my greatest pet peeves as a high school instructor sheerly due to its regularity in student writing. The problem is not that students ignore capitalization in texts—I don't begrudge them that freedom. Rather, it's that they allow those habits to carry over into settings like the workplace or the classroom. College- and career-ready people have simply learned how to avoid doing that.

PUNCTUATE PERFECTLY

Nothing says "Throw me into the slush pile" to a prospective employer like a cover letter with a few run-ons or fragments. College- and career-ready people dominate punctuation. They know, *either instinctively or consciously*, the difference between a clause and a phrase, between a subordinating and a coordinating conjunction, between a dependent and an independent clause. This provides them with a solid working knowledge of how sentences work, and they use this understanding to appropriately place commas and periods and other punctuation of this ilk.

SPELL SUPERBLY

If there's anything that lands cover letters in the slush pile with greater frequency than poorly placed punctuation, it has got to be misspellings. You don't need to be a Scripps National Spelling Bee champion to be college and career ready, but you do need to be able to correctly spell high-frequency homophones—computer-based spell-checkers still can't consistently catch these errors—and have a strong grasp of the spelling patterns of English. To shore up any shortcomings in those two areas, you had better know how to look up words you're unsure of.

WHY IS THIS IMPORTANT?

Most rubrics in school give "conventions" one of several seats at the table of traits of great writing. Unfortunately, the world of work is not so kind—although that email to the boss may be rife with keen insight and well-organized thought, it is unlikely to impress her if the writer can't avoid distracting capitalization, punctuation, or spelling errors. A professional who shows up to work on Monday in shabby dress is unlikely to thrive within the company, and a writer who consistently makes surface-level errors in his writing is likely to find few promotions heading his way. This may seem superficial, but it is also the truth. We are being kind when we tell our students as much and then give them the tools to become conventional writers.

The 3rd college and career readiness anchor standard within the language strand of the CCSS reads as follows:

> Apply knowledge of language to understand how language functions in different contexts, to make effective choices for meaning or style, and to comprehend more fully when reading or listening.

In other words, college- and career-ready students understand how language works in various settings (for example, in work and in academia), and they leverage this understanding both to make powerful decisions about style and usage and to comprehend more fully the language they receive from others.

USING THE GRADE-SPECIFIC REQUIREMENTS TO GAIN A DEEPER UNDERSTANDING OF THE ANCHOR

Although this anchor makes general sense, it is initially difficult to discern what exact skills it comprises. This is where the grade-specific standards come in handy; they help us flesh out a more comprehensive picture of what college and career readiness looks like for a given standard. In the case of L.CCR.3, here are some sample skills drawn from the grade-specific skill descriptions (some of these are repeated from our look at the grade-specific standards in L.CCR.1; I include them in this list to give a sense of the variety of moves specific to this standard):

Grade 2: "Compare formal and informal uses of English" (L.2.3.A).

Grade 3: "Choose words and phrases for effect" (L.3.3.A).

Grade 4: "Differentiate between contexts that call for formal English (e.g., presenting ideas) and situations where informal discourse is appropriate (e.g., small group discussion)" (L.4.3.C).

Grade 5: "Expand, combine, and reduce sentences for meaning, reader/listener interest, and style" (L.5.3.A).[1]

Grade 6: "Maintain consistency in style and tone" (L.6.3.B).

Grade 7: "Choose language that expresses ideas precisely and concisely, recognizing and eliminating wordiness and redundancy" (L.7.3.A).

Grade 8: "Use verbs in the active and passive voice and in the conditional and subjunctive mood to achieve particular effects (e.g., emphasizing the actor or the action; expressing uncertainty or describing a state contrary to fact)" (L.8.3.A).

Grades 9–10: "Write and edit work so that it conforms to the guidelines in a style manual...appropriate for the discipline and writing type" (L.9–10.3.A).

Grades 11–12: "Vary syntax for effect, consulting references...for guidance as needed; apply an understanding of syntax to the study of complex texts when reading" (L.11–12.3.A).

Let's examine a few of the general language skills that this anchor standard aims at.

HOW DOES LANGUAGE FUNCTION IN DIFFERENT CONTEXTS?

College- and career-ready people know there are specific changes they must make to the language they use if they are to communicate effectively in a given setting. For example, in a history course, arguments and explanatory pieces are in the past tense, whereas in a

---

1. The simplest approach to these skills comes in the form of Don Killgallon's *Sentence Composing* series of texts (1997, 1998a, 1998b; Killgallon & Killgallon, 2000), which span from the elementary level to the college level.

literature course, arguments are written in the present tense. Some courses require papers to be written using MLA format; others require APA. In most careers, wordiness and redundancy are considered unprofessional and unproductive—people want to read and listen to efficient, communicative language.

HOW DO I USE LANGUAGE TO COMMUNICATE AND COMPREHEND EFFECTIVELY?

A college- and career-ready person's knowledge of language improves his communication and his comprehension. When communicating, he gets to the point as directly and clearly as possible, choosing language that avoids redundancy and wordiness, and when listening or reading, he is able to sort through both high- and low-quality language to determine what the speaker or writer is seeking to communicate. As this awareness of language grows, the college- and career-ready person develops the ability to make effective stylistic choices that help him not only communicate ideas but also move his audience to reflection or action.

WHY IS THIS IMPORTANT?

Students struggle with understanding this standard due to its abstract nature. Because of this, I tell my students that, if this were a *Star Wars* film and language were the Force, then this standard would be about using one's overarching understanding of the Force to navigate novel situations with style and ease. When language becomes something we grasp as a communicative tool, we begin to see language use as a set of choices, and this empowers us to make our choices good ones.

L.CCR.
4

The 4th college and career readiness anchor standard within the language strand of the CCSS reads as follows:

> Determine or clarify the meaning of unknown and multiple-meaning words and phrases by using context clues, analyzing meaningful word parts, and consulting general and specialized reference materials, as appropriate.

Here's the short version: college- and career-ready people are good word figure-outers. In other words, L.CCR.4 is all about one central question: What do you do when you encounter words you don't know? The anchor standard answers this central question with three main strategies for figuring out word meanings.

USE CONTEXT CLUES

College- and career-ready people need to know how to gather information about an unfamiliar word using the words around it. Although this is the quickest way to determine the meaning of an unfamiliar word, it does have its limitations, especially when reading texts with an abundance of unfamiliar words. With texts like that, it's best to verify the inferred meaning with an external reference. From a teaching perspective, the easiest way to model a nuanced application and understanding of using context clues to determine word meaning is through modeling our own thinking during a read-aloud of a complex text.

ANALYZE WORD PARTS

Suffixes, prefixes, and root words—booyah! Analysis, remember, is simply pulling a thing apart and then "look[ing] closely at each of its parts and see[ing] if they fit together in a way that makes sense" (Marzano & Simms, 2013, p. 76). When students learn the meanings of high-frequency word parts, they become readers who approach unfamiliar words as intriguing puzzles rather than as insurmountable obstacles. Because of this, the grade-specific versions of L.CCR.4 have kids learning word parts even in the earliest grades; by the time fifth grade comes, they're familiar with some basic Greek and Latin roots; by twelfth grade, they are beginning to use patterns of word changes to infer more nuanced levels of meaning (for example, they begin to understand how and why the words "analyze," "analysis," and "analytical" are related and different).

USE REFERENCES

Dictionaries, glossaries, thesauruses, and etymological references become more than dusty volumes or unclicked Internet bookmarks for college- and career-ready people. Such reference materials help these lifelong learners to gain an understanding of words they can't define using the previous two methods and to clarify inferences made using one or both of the previous methods. These references have specific uses in the college- and career-ready person's mind (for example, a thesaurus can help me get an idea of a word through reading about similar words, but it's not as precise as a dictionary).

WHY IS THIS IMPORTANT?

With over five million words in the English language, college- and career-ready people are word learners who know when and how to grapple with words they don't know. This ability empowers them to do the voracious reading and listening required to be adaptable and employable in today's economies. To help motivate my students to be the kinds of people who naturally apply these strategies to unknown words, I love sharing with them excerpts from E. D. Hirsch Jr.'s article "A Wealth of Words" (2013), which discusses the correlations between vocabulary size and income. In short, it pays to be a person who habitually determines the meanings of unfamiliar words.

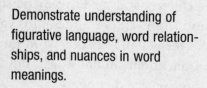

L.CCR. 5

The 5th college and career readiness anchor standard within the language strand of the CCSS reads as follows:

> Demonstrate understanding of figurative language, word relationships, and nuances in word meanings.

Essentially, this standard gets at answering one question: What do we do when the literal words on the page are not intended to communicate what the dictionary says about them? What do we do when authors or speakers use nonliteral language for effect?

MEANING ONE THING, SAYING ANOTHER

I jokingly refer to this as the "Bradbury standard" because, as a freshman English teacher in my high school, I read Ray Bradbury's *Fahrenheit 451* (1953) with my students each year, a novel more replete with nonliteral language than any text I've ever read. On the first page of the novel, readers encounter a serpent that's actually a hose, venom that's actually kerosene, and an orchestra conductor who's actually a pyromaniac fireman.

And this is just the figurative language. Throughout the rest of the book, readers must grapple with nuanced word usage; odd word relationships; and a truckload of similes, metaphors, and allusions on every page.

Some of my freshman students quickly cry foul. "When, in real life, will we encounter such roundabout language?" they ask.

I'm ready for this question with a recent column: Leonard Pitts Jr.'s, "One Man's Fix to End Politics as Usual" (2012). In the editorial, Pitts uses these related words: "crusade," "quixotic," "undaunted," "mission," "driven," and "tilting at windmills." Separately, the meanings of these terms can be ascertained using the skills of L.CCR.4, but taken together, they are meant to bring to mind Don Quixote and to thereby implicitly paint Robert Kilmer as an outmatched but pure-hearted knight of contemporary U.S. politics.

WHY IS THIS IMPORTANT?

Any experienced teacher knows that not all students will buy into the need for this anchor's skills simply from being shown an editorial column about politics. To be college and career ready, however, there's no way around the simple truth that nonliteral language is employed by expert communicators, and if we want to understand these people and their words deeply, we've got to develop these skills. At the same time, not all of the Common Core anchor standards are created equal, and so I honestly spend more time on L.CCR.4 and L.CCR.6 than I do on L.CCR.5, simply because I think the former are more critical. After all, if students aren't able to determine what "quixotic" means, the word relationships employed in Pitts's article will be lost on them.

L.CCR.

6

The 6th college and career readiness anchor standard within the language strand of the CCSS reads as follows:

> Acquire and use accurately a range of general academic and domain-specific words and phrases sufficient for reading, writing, speaking, and listening at the college and career readiness level; demonstrate independence in gathering vocabulary knowledge when encountering an unknown term important to comprehension or expression.

The Common Core authors saved their lengthiest anchor standard for last, and it's a biggie. Essentially, this one is about becoming an autonomous vocabulary builder.

EFFECTIVELY ACQUIRE AND USE A RANGE OF GENERAL ACADEMIC AND DOMAIN-SPECIFIC VOCABULARY

To understand this anchor, it's useful to know that the Common Core document subscribes to a three-tier model of conceptualizing categories of words that college- and career-ready people need to master (see Table L.CCR.6.1). I find it useful to explicitly teach these tiers to my freshman students to help them think strategically about their respective lexicons. They are often surprised to find that the words they usually think of as hard words are Tier 3 words, and that these words are often easier to pay attention to—and thus learn—than Tier 2 words. The tricky thing about Tier 2 words is that they transcend disciplines, and thus no discipline fully takes ownership of teaching them to students. As a result, I try to impress on my students the importance of becoming people who habitually seek vocabulary knowledge about non-discipline-specific words.

TABLE L.CCR.6.1 THREE TIERS OF WORDS

Tier 1	These are "the words of everyday speech usually learned in the early grades, albeit not at the same rate by all children. They are not considered a challenge to the average native speaker, though English language learners of any age will have to attend carefully to them. While Tier One words are important, they are not the focus of this discussion."
Tier 2 (referred to in L.CCR.6 as general academic words)	These words are "far more likely to appear in written texts than in speech. They appear in all sorts of texts: informational texts (words such as *relative*, *vary*, *formulate*, *specificity*, and *accumulate*), technical texts (*calibrate*, *itemize*, *periphery*), and literary texts (*misfortune*, *dignified*, *faltered*, *unabashedly*). Tier Two words often represent subtle or precise ways to say relatively simple things—*saunter* instead of *walk*, for example. Because Tier Two words are found across many types of texts, they are highly generalizable."
Tier 3 (referred to in L.CCR.6 as domain-specific words)	These words "are specific to a domain or field of study (*lava*, *carburetor*, *legislature*, *circumference*, *aorta*) and key to understanding a new concept within a text. Because of their specificity and close ties to content knowledge, Tier Three words are far more common in informational texts than in literature. Recognized as new and 'hard' words for most readers (particularly student readers), they are often explicitly defined by the author of a text, repeatedly used, and otherwise heavily scaffolded (e.g., made a part of a glossary)."

Source: All quotations derived from National Governors Association Center for Best Practices & Council of Chief State School Officers. (2010). *Common Core State Standards for English language arts and literacy in history/social studies, science, and technical subjects.* Washington, DC: Author, 33.

INDEPENDENTLY AND STRATEGICALLY GATHER KNOWLEDGE WHEN FACED WITH AN IMPORTANT UNKNOWN WORD

The anchor lays out two situations in which a college- and career-ready person will always gather missing vocabulary knowledge: when the word is important to comprehension, or when the word is important to expression. First of all, college- and career-ready readers know that not all unknown words inhibit comprehension. When my students read Homer's *The Odyssey*, I model for them how I differentiate between words that are curious and words that are critical. For example, in one episode of Odysseus's adventures, the men come upon the island of Helios's special cattle, and Homer includes some specific information about Helios's cowherds. Even though this information contains words I'm unfamiliar with, I move through it as a reader without gathering more information about the words because my hunch is that such information will not be necessary to comprehending the episode. When I do this, I model for my students the importance of honing the ability to ascertain which words aren't critical for comprehending a given text.

The bar is a bit higher when considering the use of an unknown word in our written or spoken expression. Unlike when reading, where my decision to gather information about a word or not affects only my understanding of the text, if I start using unknown words in my own communication with others, I'm bound to confuse my audience or look like a knucklehead—or both. Basically, college- and career-ready people aren't those who use big words in writing or speaking while lacking a clear idea of what they mean, because nobody except time-constrained teachers tends to reward this kind of communicating.

WHY IS THIS IMPORTANT?

Common Core's Appendix A makes a strong case for this anchor's inclusion as a college and career readiness skill:

> The importance of students acquiring a rich and varied vocabulary cannot be overstated. Vocabulary has been empirically connected to reading comprehension since at least 1925 (Whipple, 1925) and had its importance to comprehension confirmed in recent years (National Institute of Child Health and Human Development, 2000). It is widely accepted among researchers that the difference in students' vocabulary levels is a key factor in disparities in academic achievement (Baumann & Kameenui, 1991; Becker, 1977; Stanovich, 1986) but that vocabulary instruction has been neither frequent nor systematic in most schools (Biemiller, 2001; Durkin, 1978; Lesaux, Kieffer, Faller, & Kelley, 2010; Scott & Nagy, 1997). (National Governors Association Center for Best Practices & Council of Chief State School Officers, 2010, p. 33)

CONCLUSION

ONE NON–FREAKED OUT APPROACH TO IMPLEMENTING THE STANDARDS

When I set out in June 2012 to blog through the Common Core State Standards (CCSS), I was a die-hard standards avoider. To me, standards were nothing more than codified wish lists created by committee. They were useful for getting good grades on School of Ed lesson plans, and that was the extent of their value.

But the CCSS, as I discovered through blogging about much of the material in this book, are more focused than their wish list predecessors. And yet, although the 32 anchor standards are perhaps the shortest, most widely referenced list to date of what it means to possess the literacy skills needed for success after high school, there are still too many skills to teach them all well. I believe that as educators in real classrooms, we have got to be picky. With that being said, I'd advise you to take

Mike Schmoker's approach (2011) and, with your colleagues, cut this list of standards down by 50 percent. This will allow you to determine collectively which literacy skills your students most need, and then it will afford you the critical space in your curriculum and classroom to work on becoming excellent at helping students learn those particular skills.

Toward the end of helping you, I'll close the book by sharing the drastically pared down priorities that I have drawn from the Common Core and brought to bear on my history and English classes. It's probably true that no list can be perfect, but this one has produced promising results in my classroom—I offer it as a reference point for your own decisions about how you'll begin implementing the Common Core in your setting.

REGULARLY GRAPPLE WITH GRADE-LEVEL COMPLEX TEXTS

Every kid should have the opportunity to learn how to struggle with texts that are appropriately complex for his grade level. These texts often should be chosen for the student, not the other way around—this simply ensures that every kid gets access both to the opportunity to be challenged at a level appropriate for individuals on pace for college and career readiness and to the instruction necessary to help her do so. (This is basically R.CCR.10.)

For my friends who *rightly* point out that this approach could kill a child's love for reading, you can put down your weapons—I agree! I am not advocating against choice reading; book love (Kittle, 2013); or the instructionally sound practice of honoring students' "just right" levels. These are good things that make up an integral part of my English language arts curriculum. In fact, if it weren't for the book love that grows in many of my students during the more choice-heavy portion of my curriculum or in the midst of book talks throughout the school year, I would probably have fewer of them who were willing to grapple with the grade-appropriate complex texts I teach them to read independently. And yes—they do read them!

To me, giving kids this chance is a matter of equity and honesty. You see, though I teach ninth grade, some of my students can only read at an elementary level—teachers around the nation can relate to this situation. Although I require all of my kids to read choice books they find enjoyable, thus cultivating in themselves an authentic reading life, I also require them to experience the same opportunity I give my on-level and advanced readers: the chance to read the level of texts—articles, novels, plays, poems, blog posts, and so on—that ninth graders across the nation are reading. I do this because I want to be real with my kids about the world outside of our classroom; I want to show them there's more to being successful than simply enjoying reading. My students are inspired by having much expected of them (largely due to our intensive focus on character strengths, which we'll get to in a moment).

One more thing: obviously, it would be pretty jacked up if I were to give Johnny "I-Read-at-a-Fifth-Grade-Level" Johnson a copy of *Things Fall Apart* (Achebe, 1959) or an article from the *New York Times* and tell him, "Yo, read this," only to then go to my desk, put up my feet, and sip my coffee.

When I give kids complex texts, I've got to teach them how to read them. It's pointless to give students grade-level complex texts if we don't empower them with simple, effective instructional practices like modeling annotation, teaching key academic vocabulary, and checking for understanding (all of which Schmoker [2011] treats concisely in *Focus*). I'm not saying that these instructional practices are going to magically make it so Johnny J. can read *Things Fall Apart* at 100 percent comprehension and enjoyment. I am saying they are going to give him a shot at struggling and growing as best he can with a text that's within reach of someone who's on track for college and career readiness.

GO BIG ON ARGUMENT

One of the reasons reluctant readers tend to read complex texts in my classroom is that we'll be doing plenty of arguing during and after the reading, and, as my students can tell you, arguers with evidence tend to dominate the heck out of those without.

Far too few educators and administrators know the power of argument for developing an enjoyable life of the mind. For the last two years, I've sought

to internalize and roll out the vision of Gerald Graff's *Clueless in Academe* (2003) and *They Say, I Say* (Graff & Birkenstein, 2014), and my (often flawed) efforts have managed to produce students who tend to love arguing, debating, and discussing ideas and texts. One key reason why so many undervalue argument is that they associate it with anger and discord. But argument proper is something that can actually bring us together and that, as Joseph Williams and Lawrence McEnerney (n.d.) put it, helps us collaboratively "get to the bottom of things." Argument, both written and spoken, is having a radical impact on many of my students' lives.

ENSURE THAT EVERY STUDENT SPEAKS, EVERY DAY

Before you feel like I'm pointing my finger at you and saying, "You're a bad teacher because you don't do this!" let me confess that I only began requiring every student to speak in 2011, meaning that for the first five years of my career, I went against what I'm about to say.

The soul of the speaking and listening standards will be satisfied by simply requiring every student to speak, in a professional manner, every day. Many days, this is done by having students respond to questions throughout the day's lesson using think-pair-share.[1] To ensure that all students regularly get a chance to speak to the whole class, I often use index cards with students' names on them to randomly call on students after they've had a chance to practice in pairs; this allows me to formatively assess how we're doing as speakers. About once every two weeks, my students participate in a whole-class debate or argumentative discussion— thus allowing us to work on both argumentation and speaking skills. Less frequent, more formalized speaking tasks are summative speaking assess- ments; for these, I tell students what content I am looking for, and I also tell them what I'm looking for in terms of their delivery (I use Erik Palmer's PVLEGS [2011] to assess delivery; this acronym stands for **p**oise, **v**oice, **l**ife, **e**ye contact, **g**estures, and **s**peed).

WRITE LIKE CRAZY

When kids write a lot, they become not just better at writing, but better at reading as well (Graham & Hebert, 2010). Because of this, whether I'm

teaching history or English, I require my students to write frequently. Their assignments fall into one of three categories of writing (Silver, Dewing, & Perini, 2012): provisional writing, which includes quickwrites and brainstorming; readable writing, like the one-paragraph responses to essential questions that are common in my class; or polished writing, like the multidraft summative papers that come after most of our units in English and after at least one unit per trimester in world history.

It's critical, though, not only that I require students to write this much but also that I teach them how to do it. I've often found that this can most effec- tively and simply be done through the use of model pieces of writing. For example, in world history, most of our units end with the same question: Which key concept from this unit was most significant for the time period we've been studying *and* for the present day? In other words, students must choose any of our sixteen to twenty key concepts from the unit (for example, "the Enlightenment" is a popular choice for our unit on the 1700s), and they must then argue, with specific evidence and clear reasoning, why their chosen concept was most significant then and

---

1. For a simple treatment of this strategy, visit http://serc.carleton.edu/introgeo/interactive/tpshare.html or refer to Schmoker's *Focus* (2011, pp. 59, 64).

now. In their papers, they must also address at least two opposing claims. This assignment would be frustrating for my freshman students, or at least wouldn't produce great writing from them, if I didn't either create a model of this type of essay or pull an exemplar from past students' work. As my students are drafting their intros, we look at an intro from a model; as they are dealing with a counterclaim, we look at how that's been done in an exemplar essay. Because the model papers are always on a different historical time period, students are free to borrow moves from a model paper without being tempted to steal ideas.

Here's the thing: more than once at a conference, I've heard a speaker say that our students must write vastly more than we can possibly grade. I'm quick to buy into these kinds of comments because I enjoy having a life! As a rule, I only read provisional writing over students' shoulders when I'm walking around the room checking on them; I read and respond to about a quarter of the readable writing that I ask students to do (they rarely know which quarter that will be); and I am strategic with the kind of feedback I give students on their polished writing pieces. Because I never hand back copiously corrected papers to students, they get their work back faster with one to two things to work on for next time. This allows us to write like crazy without having me go crazy.

TEACH GRIT AND SELF-CONTROL

I will be surprised if noncognitive skills (what many refer to as character strengths) do not gain a large share of the education reform conversation in the decade to come. A big reason why most of my students are willing to tread the demanding paths of complex texts, close reading, arguing, mandatory speaking, and writing is that they are growing in their skill at grit and self-control.

My colleagues and I explicitly teach, model, recognize, and speak as much as we can about these two high-powered, noncognitive skills. "Grit" is Angela Duckworth's word for resilience, stick-to-itiveness, and persistence.[2] Self-control contains the skills of being prepared, resisting procrastination, paying attention, following directions, and controlling one's temper.

---

2. Duckworth's work on grit has been discussed in many settings, but perhaps the most useful place to start learning about it is her six-minute TED Talk at http://youtube/H14bBuluwB8.

The reason I add these skills to a short list of high-bang-for-your-buck standards is simple: they hugely correlate with human flourishing, and without them the Common Core is infinitely harder and more pointless. The reality is that Suzy "I'm a Freaking Genius" Smith might be rocking a 36 on the ACT as a freshman, but if she has a low tolerance for hardship or can't find a way to manage her time, she's got a great chance of quitting when she faces life's important obstacles.

WHAT WILL YOU START WITH?

This is the list I've chosen to explore thoroughly on my quest to promote the long-term flourishing of the students who pass through my classroom, but it is by no means definitively proven or the only viable path. It does, at first glance, cut out wide swaths of the CCSS. But as I've sought to grow expertise in these few key areas, I've found that a great many of the anchors we've explored in this book are addressed while in pursuit of these five strategies. Those that aren't, I would argue, just aren't worth focusing on until I become excellent at empowering students with these first five areas.

This work is still in progress, both in my classroom and in thousands more around the country. But I am convinced that, if enough educators have a solution-oriented approach to the Common Core, if we build a critical mass of us who vow never to freak out over the next standardized test but instead to doggedly pursue long-term student flourishing, the Common Core experiment can result in a step forward for schools. If you are interested in being a part of that critical mass, come let your voice be heard at the blog this book was born from, www.teachingthecore.com.

APPENDIX

ALL ANCHORS ON A 2-PAGE SPREAD

Reading

R.CCR.1 Read closely to determine what the text says explicitly and to make logical inferences from it; cite specific textual evidence when writing or speaking to support conclusions drawn from the text.

R.CCR.2 Determine central ideas or themes of a text and analyze their development; summarize the key supporting details and ideas.

R.CCR.3 Analyze how and why individuals, events, or ideas develop and interact over the course of a text.

R.CCR.4 Interpret words and phrases as they are used in a text, including determining technical, connotative, and figurative meanings, and analyze how specific word choices shape meaning or tone.

R.CCR.5 Analyze the structure of texts, including how specific sentences, paragraphs, and larger portions of the text (e.g., a section, chapter, scene, or stanza) relate to each other and the whole.

R.CCR.6 Assess how point of view or purpose shapes the content and style of a text.

R.CCR.7 Integrate and evaluate content presented in diverse media and formats, including visually and quantitatively, as well as in words.

Writing

W.CCR.1 Write arguments to support claims in an analysis of substantive topics or texts using valid reasoning and relevant and sufficient evidence.

W.CCR.2 Write informative/explanatory texts to examine and convey complex ideas and information clearly and accurately through the effective selection, organization, and analysis of content.

W.CCR.3 Write narratives to develop real or imagined experiences or events using effective technique, well-chosen details, and well-structured event sequences.

W.CCR.4 Produce clear and coherent writing in which the development, organization, and style are appropriate to task, purpose, and audience.

W.CCR.5 Develop and strengthen writing as needed by planning, revising, editing, rewriting, or trying a new approach.

W.CCR.6 Use technology, including the Internet, to produce and publish writing and to interact and collaborate with others.

W.CCR.7 Conduct short as well as more sustained research projects based on focused questions, demonstrating understanding of the subject under investigation.

Reading (continued)

R.CCR.8 Delineate and evaluate the argument and specific claims in a text, including the validity of the reasoning as well as the relevance and sufficiency of the evidence.

R.CCR.9 Analyze how two or more texts address similar themes or topics in order to build knowledge or to compare the approaches the authors take.

R.CCR.10 Read and comprehend complex literary and informational texts independently and proficiently.

Writing (continued)

W.CCR.8 Gather relevant information from multiple print and digital sources, assess the credibility and accuracy of each source, and integrate the information while avoiding plagiarism.

W.CCR.9 Draw evidence from literary or informational texts to support analysis, reflection, and research.

W.CCR.10 Write routinely over extended time frames (time for research, reflection, and revision) and shorter time frames (a single sitting or a day or two) for a range of tasks, purposes, and audiences.

Speaking and Listening

SL.CCR.1 Prepare for and participate effectively in a range of conversations and collaborations with diverse partners, building on others' ideas and expressing their own clearly and persuasively.

SL.CCR.2 Integrate and evaluate information presented in diverse media and formats, including visually, quantitatively, and orally.

SL.CCR.3 Evaluate a speaker's point of view, reasoning, and use of evidence and rhetoric.

SL.CCR.4 Present information, findings, and supporting evidence such that listeners can follow the line of reasoning and the organization, development, and style are appropriate to task, purpose, and audience.

SL.CCR.5 Make strategic use of digital media and visual displays of data to express information and enhance understanding of presentations.

SL.CCR.6 Adapt speech to a variety of contexts and communicative tasks, demonstrating command of formal English when indicated or appropriate.

Language

L.CCR.1 Demonstrate command of the conventions of standard English grammar and usage when writing or speaking.

L.CCR.2 Demonstrate command of the conventions of standard English capitalization, punctuation, and spelling when writing.

L.CCR.3 Apply knowledge of language to understand how language functions in different contexts, to make effective choices for meaning or style, and to comprehend more fully when reading or listening.

L.CCR.4 Determine or clarify the meaning of unknown and multiple-meaning words and phrases by using context clues, analyzing meaningful word parts, and consulting general and specialized reference materials, as appropriate.

L.CCR.5 Demonstrate understanding of figurative language, word relationships, and nuances in word meanings.

L.CCR.6 Acquire and use accurately a range of general academic and domain-specific words and phrases sufficient for reading, writing, speaking, and listening at the college and career readiness level; demonstrate independence in gathering vocabulary knowledge when encountering an unknown term important to comprehension or expression.

WORKS CITED

Achebe, C. (1959). *Things fall apart*. New York, NY: Anchor Books.

Adler, M., & Van Doren, C. (1972). *How to read a book: The classic guide to intelligent reading*. New York, NY: Touchstone.

Anderson, J. (2011). *Ten things every writer needs to know*. Portland, ME: Stenhouse.

Atwell, N. (2002). *Lessons that change writers*. Portsmouth, NH: Heinemann.

Baumann, J. F., & Kameenui, E. J. (1991). Research on vocabulary instruction: Ode to Voltaire. In J. Flood, J. M. Jensen, D. Lapp, & J. R. Squire (Eds.), *Handbook of research on teaching the English language arts* (pp. 604–632). New York, NY: Macmillan.

Becker, W. C. (1977). Teaching reading and language to the disadvantaged—what we have learned from field research. *Harvard Educational Review, 47*, 518–543.

Biemiller, A. (2001). Teaching vocabulary: Early, direct, and sequential. *American Educator, 25*(1), 24–28, 47.

Bloom, B. S. (1956). *Taxonomy of educational objectives: Handbook 1. The cognitive domain*. New York, NY: David McKay.

Bradbury, R. (1953). *Fahrenheit 451*. New York, NY: Simon & Schuster.

Burke, J. (2013). *The Common Core companion: The standards decoded, grades 9–12; What they say, what they mean, how to teach them*. Thousand Oaks, CA: Corwin.

Conley, D. (2014). *Getting ready for college, careers, and the Common Core: What every educator needs to know*. San Francisco, CA: Jossey-Bass.

Coplin, B. (2012). *10 things employers want you to learn in college: The skills you need to succeed*. New York, NY: Ten Speed Press.

Durkin, D. (1978). What classroom observations reveal about comprehension instruction. *Reading Research Quarterly, 14*, 481–533.

Fine, S. (2010, October 20). Moving forward with the Common Core. *Education Week*, 30, 18–19. Retrieved from http://www.edweek.org/ew/articles/2010/10/20/08fine.h30.html

Fisher, D. (2014). *Video 1.5: Doug talks about the gradual release of responsibility* [Video file]. Retrieved from http://www.corwin.com/rigorousreading/chapter.htm

Gallagher, K. (2004). *Deeper reading: Comprehending challenging texts, 4–12*. Portland, ME: Stenhouse.

Gallagher, K. (2009). *Readicide: How schools are killing reading and what you can do about it*. Portland, ME: Stenhouse.

Graff, G. (2003). *Clueless in academe: How schooling obscures the life of the mind*. New Haven, CT: Yale University Press.

Graff, G., & Birkenstein, C. (2014). *They say, I say: The moves that matter in academic writing* (3rd ed.). New York, NY: W. W. Norton.

Graham, S., & Hebert, M. A. (2010). *Writing to read: Evidence for how writing can improve reading* (Carnegie Corporation Time to Act Report). Washington, DC: Alliance for Excellent Education.

Green, J. [CrashCourse]. (2013, January 10). *Language, voice, and Holden Caulfield:* The Catcher in the Rye *part 1* [Video file]. Retrieved from http://youtube/R66eQLLOins

Hirsch, E. D., Jr. (2013, Winter). A wealth of words: The key to increasing upward mobility is expanding vocabulary. *City Journal*. Retrieved from http://www.city-journal.org/2013/23_1_vocabulary.html

Huddle, D. (1986). *Only the little bone*. Boston, MA: David R. Godine.

Killgallon, D. (1997). *Sentence composing for middle school: A worktext on sentence variety and maturity*. Portsmouth, NH: Heinemann.

Killgallon, D. (1998a). *Sentence composing for college: A worktext on sentence variety and maturity*. Portsmouth, NH: Heinemann.

Killgallon, D. (1998b). *Sentence composing for high school: A worktext on sentence variety and maturity*. Portsmouth, NH: Heinemann.

Killgallon, D., & Killgallon, J. (2000). *Sentence composing for elementary school: A worktext to build better sentences*. Portsmouth, NH: Heinemann.

Kipling, R. (1899). The white man's burden. *McClure's Magazine*, 12.

Kittle, P. (2013). *Book love: Developing depth, stamina, and passion in adolescent readers*. Portsmouth, NH: Heinemann.

Knowles, J. (1959). *A separate peace*. New York, NY: Scribner.

Lehman, C. (2012). *Energize research reading and writing: Fresh strategies to spark interest, develop independence, and meet key Common Core standards*. Portsmouth, NH: Heinemann.

Lesaux, N. K., Kieffer, M. J., Faller, S. E., & Kelley, J. G. (2010). The effectiveness and ease of implementation of an academic English vocabulary intervention for linguistically diverse students in urban middle schools. *Reading Research Quarterly*, 45, 196–228.

Marzano, R., & Simms, J. (2013). *Vocabulary for the Common Core*. Bloomington, IN: Marzano Research Laboratory.

National Commission on Writing for America's Families, Schools, and Colleges. (2004). *Writing: A ticket to work...or a ticket out*. New York, NY: College Entrance Examination Board.

National Governors Association Center for Best Practices & Council of Chief State School Officers. (2010). *Common Core State Standards for English language arts and literacy in history/social studies, science, and technical subjects*. Washington, DC: Author.

National Institute of Child Health and Human Development. (2000). *Teaching children to read: An evidence-based assessment of the scientific research literature on reading and its implications for reading instruction* (NIH Publication No. 00-4769). Washington, DC: U.S. Government Printing Office.

Orwell, G. (1945). *Animal farm*. Orlando, FL: Harcourt Brace.

Overfield, A. (2011). *The human record: Sources of global history since 1500* (7th ed.). Boston, MA: Wadsworth.

Palmer, E. (2011). *Well spoken: Teaching speaking to all students*. Portland, ME: Stenhouse.

Pitts, L., Jr. (2011, February 3). America, the stupid giant, is evolving backward. *The Press of Atlantic City*. Retrieved from http://www.pressofatlanticcity.com/opinion/commentary/leonard-pitts-jr-america-the-stupid-giant-is-evolving-backward/article_a48934e6-c110–5f50–83b4-fae01a2c071e.html

Pitts, L., Jr. (2012, August 4). One man's fix to end politics as usual. *The Miami Herald*. Retrieved from http://www.miamiherald.com/2012/07/29/2933301/one-mans-fix-to-end-politics-as.html

Remarque, E. M. (1929). *All quiet on the western front.* Boston, MA: Little, Brown.

Salinger, J. D. (1951). *The catcher in the rye.* Boston, MA: Little, Brown.

Schmoker, M. (2011). *Focus: Elevating essentials to radically improve student learning.* Alexandria, VA: ASCD.

Scott, J., & Nagy, W. E. (1997). Understanding the definitions of unfamiliar verbs. *Reading Research Quarterly, 32,* 184–200.

Shakespeare, W. (1992). *Romeo and Juliet* (Washington Square Press New Folger ed.). New York, NY: Washington Square Press.

Siegler, M. (2010). Eric Schmidt: Every 2 days we create as much information as we did up to 2003 [Blog post]. Retrieved from http://techcrunch.com/2010/08/04/schmidt-data/

Silver, H. F., Dewing, R. T., & Perini, M. J. (2012). *The core six: Essential strategies for achieving excellence with the Common Core.* Alexandria, VA: ASCD.

Smith, M., Wilhelm, J., & Fredricksen, J. (2012). *Oh, yeah?! Putting argument to work both in school and out.* Portsmouth, NH: Heinemann.

Stafford, W. (1998). Fifteen. In *The way it is: New and selected poems* (p. 106). Minneapolis, MN: Graywolf Press.

Stanovich, K. E. (1986). Matthew effects in reading: Some consequences of individual differences in the acquisition of literacy. *Reading Research Quarterly, 21,* 360–407.

Truss, L. (2003). *Eats, shoots and leaves: The zero tolerance approach to punctuation.* New York, NY: Penguin Group.

Washington, G. (1796). Washington's farewell address 1796. Retrieved from http://avalon.law.yale.edu/default.asp

Whipple, G. (Ed.). (1925). The twenty-fourth yearbook of the National Society for the Study of Education: Report of the National Committee on Reading. Bloomington, IL: Public School.

Williams, J. M., & McEnerney, L. (n.d.). *Writing in college: A short guide to college writing.* Retrieved from http://writing-program.uchicago.edu/resources/collegewriting/high_school_v_college.htm#_Toc431538572

Wolf, M. (2007). *Proust and the squid: The story and science of the reading brain.* New York, NY: HarperCollins.

INDEX

f denotes figure; *n* denotes footnote; *t* denotes table.

A

Ability levels, 57–58, 61*f*, 62
Academia, 68, 69, 73
Academic genres, 76
Academic words, 150, 151*t*
Accuracy: of research sources, 104–105; of writing, 78–79
Achebe, C., 30–32, 36, 37, 43, 45, 54, 56, 101, 156
ACT, 85
Adler, M., 54
All Quiet on the Western Front (Remarque), 38–39, 45, 100–101
"America, the Stupid Giant, Is Evolving Backward" (Pitts), 40
Anchor standards: content-area teachers' responsibilities for, 10; definition of, 10–11; focus of, 155; versus grade-level standards, 11–12; listing of, 162–163; notation for, 18; number of, 10, 21; rationale for name of, 11; significance of, 12; visual representation of, 12*f. See also* Common Core State Standards; *specific standards*
Anderson, J., 90
Animal Farm (Orwell), 15
Annotating texts: versus close reading, 22–23; to prepare for conversations, 116
Anxiety, in U.S. education, 2
Apple Keynote, 130
Argument literacy, 67
Arguments: basic parts of, 51–52; in content areas, 68–69; delineating, 51–52; description of, 68–69; evaluating, 52–53; importance of, 53, 72–74, 157; in informational texts, 75; purpose of, 67; winning, 73–74
Arguments, creating: benefits of, 72–74; example of, 69–71; graphic organizers for, 69*n*; importance of, 67–68, 71, 158–159; prevalence of, across grades, 83; students' enjoyment of, 71, 72, 73; summarization as part of, 28; text structure of, 42; versus writing informational texts, 77–78; writing process for, 88–89
Articles: linking of, 55; structure of, 39–40
Artistic media, 49
Atwell, N., 40
Audience: for speaking, 125–126, 127, 132; for writing, 86, 91, 110
Authorial approaches, 56

B

Baumann, J. F., 153
Beaton, E., 41, 41*n*, 78, 85–86, 116
Becker, W. C., 153
Belgian Congo, 46
Bias, evaluating content for, 48
Biemiller, A., 153
Birkenstein, C., 28, 40, 53, 117, 157

Blogging, xiii, 94, 96
Bloom, B. S., 72
Book love, 156
Bradbury, R., 35, 148
Brain research, 33
Burke, J., 11–12, 26, 34, 38, 49, 120, 122, 127
Buzzwords, 21–22

C

Capitalization, 141
Career growth, 73
The Catcher in the Rye (Salinger), 44, 45
CCSS. *See* Common Core State Standards
CCSSO. *See* Council of Chief State School Officers
Cedar Springs High School, 4
Central ideas (themes): author's development of, 27–28; definition of, 26; linking, 54–55
Central ideas (themes), determining: benefits of, 27–28; in college and career readiness, 29; in content areas, 26–27; description of, 26–27; importance of, 29; strategies for, 28
Character building, 72
Charity: Water, 128, 130–131
Choice, of texts, 57–58, 156
Citations, 86, 105
Civility, 72–73
Claims: definition of, 51; making, 69–70; reasoning associated with, 71; supporting, 70–71
Clarity, of writing, 78–79
Clean water campaigns, 128, 130–131
Close reading. *See* Reading closely
Clueless in Academe (Graff), 53, 107, 157
Clunky writing, 90–91
Code switching, 132
Collaboration: in creating arguments, 72; using technology for, 96–97
College and career readiness: analyzing ideas, characters, and events in, 32; analyzing point of view and purpose for, 46; analyzing words and phrases for, 37; anchor standard notation for, 18; broad skills required for, 13–17; character building for, 72; close reading and, 21, 22, 25; context of language and, 144–145; creating arguments for, 69; delineating arguments for, 51–52; determining central ideas in, 29; effective conversations and, 116; evaluating content for, 48–49; informational writing for, 78–79; integrating information and, 119–120, 121; interpreting words and phrases for, 35, 152, 153; narrative writing for, 82; punctuation skills and, 142; as rationale for anchor standards, 11; reading complex, grade-appropriate texts for, 58, 63; reading related texts for, 56; reference materials

Grit, 159–160
Guided research, 100

H

Handwriting, 96, 97
Hardships, 159–160
Harrison, S., 128, 130
Hebert, M. A., 109, 158
High-frequency word parts, 147
Hirsch, E. D., Jr., 147
History: arguments in, 68; determining central ideas in, 26–27, 28; narrative skills in, 81; point of view in, 43–44; primary source readings in, 41; research questions in, 100–101; writing prompts in, 76
Homer, 69, 152
How to Read a Book: The Classic Guide to Intelligent Reading (Adler & Van Doren), 54
Huddle, D., 27
The Human Record: Sources of Global History since 1500 (Overfield), 45–46
Humility, 72–73

I

Independence, 14
Inferences, making: close reading for, 23–24; definition of, 23
Information: gathering, 103–106, 152; integrating, 49, 50, 119–121
Informational texts, reading: determining central ideas of, 26; linking of, 55; percentage of reading tasks in, 62*t*; point of view and, 43–44, 45–46; structure of, 39–40, 41–42; text complexity of, 62–63
Informational texts, writing: anchor standard for, 75; versus argumentative writing, 77–78; arguments in, 75; description of, 75–76; genres for, 76–77; importance of, 79; prevalence of, across grades, 83; sample prompts for, 76; selecting, analyzing, and organizing content for, 78; writing process for, 89. *See also* Research
Instagram, 96–97
Integrating information: description of, 49; importance of, 50, 121; method for, 119–120; need for, 120
Interactions, analyzing, 30–32
Internet connection, 93
Internet searches, 104
Interpretations, 33–34
Introductions, 90
Invitational Summer Institute (ISI), 66
iPads, 92

K

Kameenui, E. J., 153
Kelley, J. G., 153
Keyboarding courses, 94
Keynote, 130
Kieffer, M. J., 153
Killgallon, D., 144*n*
Killgallon, J., 144*n*
King Leopold II, 45, 46
King Lobengula, 45
Kipling, R., 36, 37–38, 43, 54
Kittle, P., 156
Knowledge building: as college readiness skill, 14–15; reading related texts for, 55–56; versus skill building, 55–56
Knowles, J., 44, 55
Kumalo, N., 46

L

Language: anchor standards in, 10, 162–163; for comprehending, 145; context of, 144–145; for effective communication, 145; figurative types of, 148–149; grammar and usage standards in, 137–140; importance of, 145; vocabulary skills and, 146–147; writing convention standards in, 141–142
Language arts classes, 68
Learning, 4
Lectures, 119–120
Lehman, C., 48
Lesaux, N. K., 153
Lexile system, 62
Listening: anchor standards in, 115, 119, 162–163; in conversations, 115–118; importance of, 114, 117–118, 124
Literacy skills, 109
Literal meaning, determining, 23
Literary techniques, 82
Literature: analyzing developments and interactions in, 30–31; determining central ideas of, 27; linking texts in, 54–55; percentage of reading tasks in, 62*t*; purpose and point of view in, 44–45; text complexity of, 62–63; text structure of, 38–39, 42
Logic, 71

M

Martin, T., 55
Marzano, R., 47, 147
Mathematics, 31
McEnerney, L., 67, 72, 157
Media, evaluating, 47–50
Microsoft PowerPoint, 130
Microsoft Word, 95
Modeling: of argument delineations, 52; of close reading, 22, 23, 24; of context clues, 146; to determine literal meanings, 23; of evidence citations to support conclusions, 24; of information integration, 120; to make inferences, 24; of writing, 158–159

N

NAEP. *See Reading Framework for the 2009 National Assessment of Educational Progress*
Nagy, W. E., 153
Narrative writing: anchor standard for, 80; decrease in prevalence of, 83; definition of, 80–81; details for, 81–82; effective techniques for, 82; from experiences, 81; genres of, 80–81; importance of, 84; list of skills for, 81; sequence of events in, 82; writing process for, 89
National Commission on Writing for America's Families, Schools, and Colleges, 110–111
National Governors Association Center for Best Practices (NGA), 13, 14, 15, 30, 35, 67, 68, 75, 76, 80, 83, 153
National Institute of Child Health and Human Development, 153
National Writing Project, 66
Navy SEALs, 111
New York Times, 156
Nonliteral language. *See* Figurative meanings
Novels, 38–39, 42

O

Obama, B., 15–16, 123
Odyssey (Homer), 69–71, 152